heart strong

ELLIDY PULLIN
WITH ALLEY PASCOE

heart strong

Chumpy, Minnie & Me

hachette
AUSTRALIA

hachette
AUSTRALIA

Published in Australia and New Zealand in 2022
by Hachette Australia
(an imprint of Hachette Australia Pty Limited)
Gadigal Country, Level 17, 207 Kent Street, Sydney, NSW 2000
www.hachette.com.au

Hachette Australia acknowledges and pays our respects to the past, present and future Traditional Owners and Custodians of Country throughout Australia and recognises the continuation of cultural, spiritual and educational practices of Aboriginal and Torres Strait Islander peoples. Our head office is located on the lands of the Gadigal people of the Eora Nation.

A catalogue record for this
work is available from the
National Library of Australia

ISBN: 978 0 7336 4921 9 (paperback)

Cover and internal picture section design by Christabella Designs
Cover photograph courtesy of Thomas Wielecki
Internal and back cover photographs courtesy of Ellidy Pullin and the Pullin family collection unless otherwise specified
Typeset in 12/20pt Sabon LT Std by Kirby Jones
Printed and bound in Australia by McPherson's Printing Group

MIX
Paper | Supporting
responsible forestry
FSC® C001695

The paper this book is printed on is certified against the Forest Stewardship Council® Standards. McPherson's Printing Group holds FSC® chain of custody certification SA-COC-005379. FSC® promotes environmentally responsible, socially beneficial and economically viable management of the world's forests.

For Chumpy ♥

CONTENTS

PART THREE: WHAT BECAME

Prologue

It was a sliding doors moment. The night I met Alex 'Chumpy' Pullin, he was walking up the stairs as I was heading down. Neither one of us had planned to be at my friend's twenty-first; I was nursing a sore heart after the end of my first serious relationship and Chumpy was meant to be on a plane but had changed his flight at the last minute.

A couple of days earlier, we had passed each other on another set of stairs at Warriewood Beach on Sydney's Northern Beaches. I was running up and down the stairs, doing an impromptu bootcamp with some friends, when Chumpy came down to check out the surf. Chumpy had always been on the periphery of my friendship group. We ran in the same circles, but our worlds had never collided. I knew him as the mysterious snowboarder who travelled a lot and would randomly play music at our parties when he was in town. Chumpy wasn't from Sydney, but he spent the Australian winter training at a special gym in Narrabeen, where I lived. I didn't know much about him, except that he was hot and talented, and I wanted to know more.

Chumpy looked beautiful that day at the beach, I swear his skin glowed and his eyes sparkled. Meanwhile, I was red and sweaty from running – and a bit giddy from seeing him. I wanted to say more than hi to him, but in that moment, I couldn't form complete sentences. Later, Chumpy would tell me he had wanted to talk to me too – and I would feel giddy all over again.

My friend Laura Enever's twenty-first was onesie-themed. I wore a bright pink pyjama onesie that I had borrowed from a friend, and Chumpy was in a much cooler denim jumpsuit that made him look like a full-on mechanic, but hot. Chumpy had an electric energy about him. People were drawn to him, just like I had been on the beach and how I was at the party. It's not something that's easy to pinpoint; it's the way he walked, his effortlessness, his very presence. I wasn't the only one who saw it, everyone who met him felt the same. Chumpy was larger than life,

I always told him he was beyond this world, he radiated at a higher level like he was from a different dimension to the rest of us. When you looked into his eyes, there was a depth that was other-worldly.

In typical rom-com fashion, the night of the party, our eyes kept meeting across the room and eventually our bodies met in the middle of the dance floor. 'Wild Ones' by Flo Rida featuring Sia was playing over the speaker, but all I could hear was the sound of my heart beating. All night, we danced and talked and kissed. Later, my friends would tell me they watched me on the dance floor and saw me fall in love right in front of them.

From our first kiss on that dance floor, it was on. It felt like we were two pieces of a jigsaw puzzle that fitted together perfectly. We just clicked. Everything felt right, even the date of our first official meeting was perfect: 10/11/12. I have the date engraved on the gold pendant that my friends had made for me, which I wear around my neck every day. It has an imprint of Chumpy's fingerprint on the other side.

With Chumpy, there was no playing hard to get or waiting a certain amount of time before writing back to each other. He messaged me on Facebook (as you did in 2012) as soon as he got home from the party, in the early hours of the morning, and we didn't stop talking.

We chatted about the small stuff – his training and my university studies – and the big things – our hopes and dreams for the future. The more I learned about Chumpy, the harder I fell.

Alex Pullin: Really fun hanging out with you tonight. Bummer I'm out of here soon, but have to catch up more next time.

Ellidy Vlug: Yeah me too. Had lots of fun!!!! Would love to catch up again. When do you fly to Austria? Memory is a tad blurry haha xx

Alex Pullin: I've just arrived back home on the south coast, then I'm flying to Austria next weekend. What's your exam schedule like? Pretty hectic for the week I guess? You should maybe just come on tour with me. haha

Ellidy Vlug: Sounds like fun. Busy busy, I woke up 3 am this morning to get a start on the studying. I'm expecting a few fails. Argh!

Alex Pullin: I wish we had been so clever to work this out while I was on the Beaches for six weeks. If only I'd known, I would have worn my onesie out earlier. Haha. I might be back in Sydney for New Years. Either way, whenever we get to meet up again, I'm already looking forward to it. You have had my head spinning since last Saturday.

Ellidy Vlug: Sucks so much our timing hasn't worked out!
I'll be in New York in February and back in L.A. in May, then
Vegas for my 21st. Hopefully you can show me around.

I wanna kiss you again!!

Alex Pullin: I'll happily kiss you again in any of those places
around the world. But preferably right now.

On a night out a week later, I was reading through the
messages with my friends – as you do when you're young
and crushed-up – and they were gushing about how perfect
Chumpy was, how special he was for being so in touch
with his emotions and how good we were together.

Chumpy had flown to Victoria after the party and was
in Melbourne, preparing to head overseas for the snow
season. I was complaining to my friends that he only had
a couple of days left in the country when two of them
made an executive decision. Maia and Mel hijacked my
phone and booked me a flight to Melbourne for the
next afternoon.

'You have to be with this guy,' Maia said. 'You are
amazing together and if you don't see him before he goes,
you'll regret it.'

The next day, when my friends drove me to the airport,
I did regret one thing: how many drinks we'd had the
night before.

'What kind of weirdo books a flight interstate to see a guy she's met once?' I thought. 'Will it be awkward? What if I've built up this pen pal relationship into something it's not?' I had never been more nervous.

I didn't tell my mum or my other friends what I was doing in case they thought I was mad. I was twenty and a grown-up, but I still felt like I was doing something sneaky.

When my friends dropped me off at the departures terminal, I was like a little kid on her first day of school, full of anxiety, excitement and butterflies. I felt like a wreck after a night of dancing, and I remember spending the flight putting in eye drops to try to look semi-presentable.

As soon as I saw Chumpy waiting for me at the airport gate, all my fears disappeared. Well, almost. When we hugged, I was still shaking with nerves. But he was too! Chumpy held me until we both stopped rattling in our boots. It felt like we already knew each other because we'd been talking constantly, but being in his presence took it to a whole other level.

Then he took me back to his airport hotel room, and we didn't leave it for the next twenty-four hours. Chumpy sat on the bed and played the guitar, serenading me with songs he'd written. It could've been cheesy, but it wasn't. It felt natural. I smiled so much my face hurt. We ordered enough room service to feed a family of four and sat side by side, eating and chatting. I wanted time to stop so I could stay under the crisp white sheets with Chumpy forever.

Unfortunately, I don't have the power to warp time. The sun rose the next morning and Chumpy boarded his flight to the other side of the world for a month-long trip. Of course I was sad but, more than anything, I was blissfully happy. The connection I had with Chumpy was real and no matter the distance between us, I knew we'd be together. I felt it in my bones, in my heart and in my fingertips, which had somehow always managed to find Chumpy's hand when we were together. If I wasn't so loved up, I would have rolled my eyes at how smitten I was.

I hadn't grown up with a shining example of true love. My parents, Pete, a police sergeant turned actor and model, and Karen, also a police officer who became a seamstress and fashion designer, separated when I was one and my brother, Dave, was three. I'm glad I was too little to remember that time, because it was volatile. My brother and I lived with our mum in Narrabeen and stayed with our dad every second weekend at his house in nearby Warriewood. It was so close, I could finish dinner at one house and run to the other for dessert.

When I was eight, Mum met my stepdad. That was hard because I was so used to just Mum and Dad in my life. My stepdad and I were very different.

As a kid, you think everyone's family is the same. You assume everyone orders their cutlery drawer with the knives on the left, forks on the right and spoons in the middle because that's how your mum does it. You figure all people call swimwear swimmers because you've never heard them called togs or bathers or cossies. In the same way, I thought having divorced parents, a stepdad and a sometimes tense household was normal.

I'd never really seen true love, so how could I have known it existed?

Chumpy's version of how we met was several years before the onesie party, at the Mona Vale Hotel. Back then – before it became the bourgeois Park House, with exposed brickwork, indoor plants and barrel-aged cocktails – the Mona (as us locals called it) was a classic pub with a boisterous beer garden, sleazy sports bar and sweaty dance floor. It was where me and my friends spent all of our Thursday, Friday and Saturday nights (using fake IDs to get in and going to school hungover on Fridays). Our drink of choice was this sickly sweet cocktail slushie called the Purple Sneaker. It was there, at the Mona, where Chumpy told me he first saw me.

'You were wearing a blue velvet jacket,' he'd say. My mum had made me that jacket and I wore it everywhere in my late teens, running amok with my friends, young and dancing like nobody was watching. Chumpy told me he spotted me through the crowd one night when he'd just started coming to the Northern Beaches to train at his gym. Apparently he tried to talk to me at the bar – and I gave him nothing. I would have been totally oblivious, too busy having fun with my friends, being a brat and not caring about boys.

It still makes my heart flutter to think of Chumpy sliding up next to me at the bar and brushing up against my velvet jacket, and that he remembered the moment all those years before so clearly. We'd both known of each other before we'd properly met, but I'd had no idea Chumpy was as aware of me as I was of him.

If you believe in the universe having a plan, it's easy to think our orbits were always meant to collide. We came close so many times before the night we crashed into one another and didn't let go.

Chumpy learned to love from his parents, Chris and Sally, who simply adore and cherish each other. I'd never met a couple so *together* until I met Chumpy's parents in 2013, at their home in Eden on the New South Wales south coast. Suddenly, all of Chumpy's passion and devotion made complete sense. He looked at me the same way his dad looked at his mum. He wanted to know every inch of my soul in the same way his mum knew the intricate details of his dad's mind, the calluses on his palms and the frown lines on his forehead.

We came from starkly different backgrounds. Chumpy spent the Christmas of 2013 with his family in Eden, and I stayed on the Northern Beaches in Sydney. I imagined the four of them – Chris, Sal, Chump and his sister, Emma – carefully opening their presents and reading their cards from each other. Meanwhile, I spent the day with my dad, eating Hungry Jack's for Christmas lunch. Dave was working so Dad and I took him a Whopper meal. I know that Christmas was very different to many other people's, but I loved that day with Dad. I didn't tell Chumpy about it for years because I was embarrassed about how low-key our Christmas was compared to his.

As close as Chump was with his parents, he was even closer to Emma. They played music together, wrote lyrics and shared a secret sibling language of raised eyebrows and stifled smiles. The Pullins' sense of family was like nothing I'd ever known.

Chumpy grew up above a ski hire shop in Mansfield, near Mount Buller. The family didn't have much, but they had each other. Chris and Sally would work hard through the snow season in the hopes of being able to afford a family holiday sailing during the summer. Chumpy loved the snow, but he also loved the sea. As a kid, he was more fish than human. He pretty much learned to swim before he walked, and grew up rowing, sailing and steering boats. Em called him 'Brother Fish', which seems ironic now. If only Chumpy could have breathed underwater.

Chris and Sally did everything for their kids and encouraged Chumpy's love of snowboarding, even when times were tough and money was tight. They were never short of time or love for their kids, and that shone through Chumpy. He inherited his dad's curiosity, sense of adventure and love of the ocean and his mum's love of music and native birds. From both of them he learned a connection to nature and how to love deeply.

He saw the way his parents loved each other unconditionally, and he in turn learned to love unconditionally. Chumpy's parents taught him how to treat a partner: with care, honesty and generosity. They weren't rules written down on a blackboard; they were traits taught through actions.

Chumpy loved with his whole heart. And I still can't believe I'm the girl his heart chose.

Whether we met on a set of stairs at a warehouse party or at the bar of the Mona Vale Hotel, we were drawn together for a reason. And whether I was wearing a borrowed pink onesie or the blue velvet jacket my mum made me, it was love at first sight when I saw Chumpy and he saw me.

I still have the jacket. I don't have Chumpy.

Introduction

'If we could breathe underwater
We could travel by land
Round the whole world'

— Alex 'Chumpy' Pullin lyrics, 2016

On a clear day, you can see the line where the ocean hits the horizon from our bedroom window. Chumpy was standing at the window, examining that line, when I woke up on the day the world stopped.

It was a winter's day – Wednesday 8 July 2020 – but no-one told the sun that. It beat down on the perfectly still sea. The ocean was like glass, and it called to Chumpy. He excitedly got ready to go spearfishing while I soaked up the morning sunshine from our bed.

Chumpy almost went surfing, but decided to spearfish instead. It was his latest obsession. He'd spend hours out at the Palm Beach Reef near our house on the Gold Coast, catching flathead and kingfish that we'd turn into fish tacos for dinner.

Chumpy was meticulous, and he approached spearfishing with the same dedication he put into everything else he did. He'd practise meditating in our lap pool and hold his breath with my brother at the kitchen table while I sat bored for three or so minutes.

Every time Chumpy went for a dive, I'd say, 'Love you, watch out for sharks.' He wasn't afraid of sharks. In fact, a week earlier, when his parents were visiting us on the Gold Coast, Chumpy had said as much to his dad while showing him his diving gear. Sharks weren't the worry, he said. They saw sharks all the time at Palm Beach. The hidden danger was actually shallow water blackouts. These happen when the body blacks out at the end of a breath-hold dive, and the victim either takes in water and drowns or simply loses the ability to breathe.

I was never afraid for Chumpy when he was in the water because I knew how long he could hold his breath for, I knew how careful he was, and I knew how fit he was. Chumpy was a professional athlete, for god's sake; he knew the limits of his body like the freckles on the back of his hands. He grew up in the water and he loved nothing more than being in it. The ocean gave him life, and I didn't think for a second that it would take that same life away.

The weather planned the morning for us. Chumpy was going to go for a dive to catch dinner for the friends we had visiting from Sydney that night, I was going to walk our kelpie, Rummi, and we were going to meet up after for brunch at one of our favourite cafés. We left home at the same time. Chumpy was reversing the van out of our driveway and I was standing at the garage door. We locked eyes and I made a motion with my hands, asking if he was going to shut the garage door or if he wanted me to. Instead of answering, Chumpy kept staring at me from the driver's seat of the van.

I threw my hands up in the air, feigning frustration.

Chumpy jumped out of the van and walked towards me. 'What are you going on about with those hands of yours?' he said, pulling me in to a big hug.

I melted into him one last time and then said quickly, 'Alright, have fun. See you in a bit.'

When we eventually parted, we both left the house with smiles on our faces, Chumpy headed down to the beach, me and Rummi going the other way, towards the park. I can't remember who ended up closing the garage door.

When I think back on our last interaction, my mind is blurry. No matter how many times I replay that morning in my head, it never gets clearer. I search and I search, but I never find new details hidden in the background. I pray and I pray, but I can't go back in time and never let Chumpy out of my arms.

There is one bolt of clarity in the fogginess of my memories. On my walk home from the park with Rummi, I had a sudden stabbing pain in my chest. I'd never felt anything like it before. The sharpness stopped me in my tracks, knocking the wind out of me and almost forcing me to my knees.

I clenched my heart and Rummi looked up at me as if to say, 'What the hell, Mum! Are you okay?' After thirty seconds, I was. I brushed the pain off as anxiety – maybe I needed more sleep, or some vitamins or a massage – and kept walking.

By the time I got home twenty minutes later, I'd forgotten all about it. My mum was at the house when we got back. I'd called her when we were at the park to ask if she could come over and help me clean the place before our friends arrived. Mum was upstairs tackling the bathroom and I went to start vacuuming. It was a perfectly boring Wednesday morning.

Until it wasn't.

I was cutting the fringe tassels from the rug in the lounge room when there was a knock at the front door. I poked my head around the corner and saw our neighbour Belinda standing there. That wasn't unusual. We were always chatting over the fence and popping by to each other's places. What was unusual was the tone of Belinda's voice; it sounded serious, dripping with worry.

I put the scissors down and walked to the front door, where Belinda told me that she'd just seen a Facebook post on the local community diving page about an unconscious man being pulled from the water at Palm Beach. It was awful news, but not totally out of the ordinary when you live by the beach. A week or two earlier, an older man had had a heart attack on the beach, and I imagined something similar had happened.

'How sad,' I thought, thanking Belinda for letting me know and going back to the very important task of trimming the rug.

Five minutes later, it hit me. Holy shit, it was Chump.

The realisation brought me to my feet. 'Mum, get in the car! We've got to go!' I screamed upstairs. Mum hadn't heard Belinda stop by, so she had no idea what was going on until I tried to explain things in the car on the four-minute drive down to 19th Avenue, the cul-de-sac that led down to the beach where Chumpy went diving.

'Belinda came over and said someone had been pulled out of the water at Palm Beach,' I told Mum. 'It wouldn't be Chumpy, would it? Chumpy would be the one saving the guy, wouldn't he? It wouldn't be him, would it?' I kept asking the same question over and over. Mum kept saying she didn't know. She was eerily serious, as though she went into autopilot and her police training took over.

Mum's calmness felt like a stark contrast to the commotion we drove into. There was a crowd at 19th Avenue, including paramedics, police and firefighters. Mum didn't bother to park the car. She stopped in the middle of the street and started running down to the beach. I couldn't get my legs to work. It felt like I was wading through toffee.

I slowly walked towards the scene unfolding in front of me. Every muscle in my body screamed at me to turn around and walk away, but I kept taking small, slow steps forward.

I could see a group of people on the beach a fair way back from the water's edge, and I immediately looked away. Whatever was happening down there, I didn't want to see it. I couldn't see it. I refused.

I started making up a narrative in my head. I told

myself that even if it was Chump lying on the sand, he'd be okay. Maybe his hand had been bitten off by a shark, or maybe he was unconscious and had to spend a few days in hospital. He might be hurt, but he'd be okay. He was always okay. He had to be okay.

A police officer was standing on his own near his car at the end of the cul-de-sac.

'Hey, what's happening?' I asked him, not really wanting to know the answer. 'My partner is diving out there, so we've come down because we heard something happened.'

'Does your partner have any tattoos?' the police officer asked.

I didn't want to answer him. 'Yeah, he's got some tattoos on his arms,' I said, taking a beat to remember he'd just gotten a new one. 'And an axe on his ribs.'

The police officer didn't say anything. He didn't need to. The look in his eyes told me everything. He turned away from me and refused to meet my gaze again. I turned to face the beach and saw my mum coming towards me, her face white and her eyes wide. Her steps were rigid and the stiffness of her body told me the same story the police officer told me with his eyes.

She didn't say the words out loud, but she nodded and I knew.

It was Chumpy.

Mum held on to me and led me back to her car. The police had told her to park at the surf club next door and meet them there. It must have only taken a minute, but it felt like a lifetime. We drove in silence, but my mind was screaming. The thoughts weren't rational.

I remember thinking, 'This is bullshit. We're busy today. Chump has a meeting this afternoon and I've got acupuncture. He knows that. We've got things to do. This is really inconvenient. Chumpy needs to stop whatever this nonsense is and get on with the day.'

The surf club has a big balcony that overlooks the beach. I didn't dare go near it; I didn't want to see what was happening. Instead, I sat down inside as far away from the windows as I could. Two police officers asked me a list of questions – Where do you live? What does your partner do? Where does he usually go spearfishing? How old is he? How old are you? What did you two do this morning? – and I answered them as if we were having a completely normal conversation.

I had my own questions, but I refused to ask them. I didn't want to know what had happened or where Chumpy was or if he was okay. I certainly didn't want to know if he was dead. I was hanging onto the hope of the things unsaid. If I didn't ask – and no-one told me – maybe it wouldn't be true.

I couldn't tell you how long I sat in the surf club for. My body was there, but I wasn't. I was in a state of shock and total disbelief. I wasn't distraught or hysterical; I was completely still in the midst of the mayhem. Eventually, a police officer came up to me and it was like I woke up.

'You need to call his family,' the police officer said. 'It's going to be on the news within the next couple of hours. You need to tell them.'

'What am I telling them? What happened? Is Chumpy ... not alive?' I said, unable to say the word 'dead' out loud.

I clutched my phone to my chest, pushing myself to dial Chumpy's parents' number. They didn't answer. I tried his sister. She didn't answer. Randomly, they were on the phone to each other at that exact moment, oblivious to what was happening on the sand at Palm Beach.

When they each got missed call messages from me, they hung up on their conversation. Chumpy's parents called me back.

'Something bad has happened,' I said. 'It's Chumpy.'

They asked me what had happened, but I couldn't tell them. 'I don't know. I think he's hurt,' I managed to say before I handed my phone over to the police officer to say what I couldn't.

I was crouched down on the surf club tiles when my brother arrived. Chump was like a brother to him. Dave squatted down next to me and held me tighter than I've ever been held. We both fell to the floor, but he didn't let go. I was shaking in his arms. When Mum grabbed Dave and took him downstairs, I stayed where I was. I didn't want to know what was happening downstairs. Mum told me later – much later – that they'd both said goodbye to Chumpy in the back of the ambulance. Mum hugged him and kissed him and told him how much we all loved him.

After the surf club, I only remember the logistics. Mum drove us back to my house in her car, and Dave found our van that Chumpy had driven to the beach and brought it back. Chumpy had left his wallet and phone inside it. There were missed calls on his phone from me and a bunch of his friends who'd somehow heard a tragic rumour that turned out to be true. My phone was blowing up with messages and calls too, so much so that my brother took it off me.

I needed to do something with my hands. Like a total zombie, I went back to cutting the tassels on the rug. The fucking tassels!

When Dave handed me my phone back later, I messaged my two closest friends on the Gold Coast, Chloe and Lizzo, who was like a little sister to Chump. I wrote out a message – *Chumpy died* – then deleted it. Rewrote it – *Chumpy died* – then deleted it again.

Type, backspace, type, backspace. I couldn't say what was happening. It felt wrong, rude even. I couldn't call them because speaking the words felt too real. In the end, I wrote, *Chumpy passed away this morning.* It still didn't feel right. 'Passing away' was something old people did in their sleep, not something that happened to young, fit men who left home in the morning to go spearfishing and didn't come back; not something that happened to Chumpy.

At first, I think Chloe and Lizzo must have thought I was playing some sick prank. When they realised I wasn't, they both rushed over to my house. The noise Lizzo made when she hugged me was animalistic. She didn't just cry, she howled. It shook me to my core. I still hadn't been able to shed a tear. The shock was overriding the unimaginable sadness. Lizzo's wailing made things real. I didn't have to keep asking what had happened anymore. I knew for certain Chumpy was gone – he wasn't coming back – and we'd never find out exactly what happened out at Palm Beach Reef on that stunning winter's morning.

From what I've been able to piece together, a surfer spotted Chumpy's diving buoy bobbing above the water in an unusual way and paddled over, where he saw a body under the water, still weighed down with his diving belt, lifeless. The surfer dragged him back to the beach and called for help. The local lifesavers and then the paramedics spent forty-five minutes doing CPR on him, but it was no use. Chumpy was pronounced dead by the paramedics at 11.15 am. His death certificate lists the cause of death as drowning. I like to think that he simply went to sleep under the water. He didn't struggle or fight for air or choke with panic; he simply closed his eyes and didn't open them again.

I remind myself that Chumpy died doing something that he loved in the place he loved the most: the ocean. It's cold comfort, but it's something.

The speargun, fins and weight-belt Chumpy was wearing that day are sitting in our garage. They had to cut his wetsuit off, so I didn't want it back. That's not something I could have faced seeing, knowing it was the last thing that touched his skin.

This is the story I tell of that day. I don't remember anything else about it beyond this story. I can't remember if Chumpy made me a morning coffee like he usually did, or if I listened to a podcast on my walk with Rummi, or the exact time I said goodbye to my soulmate forever. The police couldn't tell us an exact time of death, but it would have had to have been around the time I was walking home from the park with Rummi, around the time I felt that sharp pain in my chest that stopped me in my tracks. Looking back, I think that was the moment Chumpy left this Earth – the moment my heart shattered.

On a different stretch of coast, hundreds of kilometres south of Palm Beach, on Victoria's Mornington Peninsula, Chumpy's best friend, Cam Bolton, had his own emergency in the ocean on the morning of 8 July. He'd been out surfing with a young mate for a few hours when the sixteen-year-old cut his head open on the reef. The blood rushed out of the wound and turned the water red. When they got to the shore, Cam applied pressure to the young bloke's head and loaded him into the car to take him to hospital. It was only when he got into the driver's seat and grabbed his phone to find the quickest route to hospital that he saw he had sixty missed calls and a hundred messages. On another beach far away, Cam's best friend had died.

On his way home from the hospital after making sure the young bloke was alright, Cam had to pull over. He couldn't see the road for the tears in his eyes. He was an absolute wreck. By the power of tears, not by design, Cam had pulled up at the beach as the sun was setting. That's where he called me.

I don't remember what we said to each other. There were no words. He had lost his best friend and I had lost my love.

We all have a story from that day. One of our friends was in a convenience store in Bali when she got a message with the news. She screamed so loud that people outside the shop thought a horrific crime was being committed. She screamed. I was silent.

I've told my story of the day over and over again, but it still doesn't feel real. Most of my memories of this day are gone, the details have faded out of my reach. All I have left is this story. This stupid story I wish I didn't have to tell.

This is the story I tell of that day, but the story of Chumpy is so much more. To tell it, we need to go back to the beginning. We need to go back to The Before.

PART ONE

The Before

'I don't care wherever you are,
so far will never be too far'

**– Alex 'Chumpy' Pullin and Emma Pullin
'Banksia', lyrics by Love Charli, 2003**

CHAPTER ONE

About A Girl

There's a well-known rule for surfers at Narrabeen Beach: locals only. Tourists aren't welcome, including surfers from the surrounding suburbs, even if they're from nearby Warriewood to the north or Collaroy to the south. The lines are clear, and they shouldn't be crossed. That's how people get their heads kicked in.

Dave and I were allowed to surf there because we lived in Narrabeen, but our dad, who lived just down the road in Warriewood, would've been given a hard time. He wasn't a 'real' local, even though his house was almost as close to the beach as ours.

My childhood was marked by these divided lines in the sand. Mum lived in Narrabeen, Dad lived in Warriewood, and we met at a community centre in Dee Why every fortnight for Mum to hand us over for Dad's scheduled weekend visit. We had to meet on neutral ground. Borderlines shouldn't be crossed. If we were with Dad we didn't dare talk about Mum, and if we were with Mum we wouldn't talk about Dad. It was sad and I wish it wasn't that way, but it was.

Mum and Dad's relationship was tumultuous, at times they couldn't be in the same room, let alone have a civilised conversation. Dad remembers the day Mum left him, like a scene out of a movie. She packed us kids into the car – my little feet would have been dangling out of my car seat – and drove away without a word. Dad chased the car down the street throwing out questions, 'Where are you going? What are you doing?'

The separation was bound to happen. They were so different, it's hard to see how they were ever together in the first place. Chump would often say to me, 'Wow, I just can't believe those two ever even dated.' Mum was perfectly put together and once they had kids she was committed to raising a family, while Dad was a renegade rogue who wasn't a fan of routine, especially if it got in the way of an adventure. When they were together, Mum must have felt like she had three kids to look after. She would get calls from friends, saying, 'Um, I think I've just seen your two little kids sitting on the sand alone while Pete's out in the surf. You might want to come and get them.'

Pete Vlug had a reputation for being the Crocodile Dundee of the Northern Beaches. He was always nursing birds back to life or catching snakes in peoples' houses or cooking up roadkill for dinner. My dad taught me and all my friends how to surf when we were young – every Saturday was Surf Safari Day for us as Dad found the best waves to practise on – and I remember one Saturday when he found a pregnant snake at the beach. He put her in a bag and brought her home in his car full of squealing young girls, and we lived with all those baby snakes for a few months.

I don't know if there was a tipping point or if things just built up until the moment of no return, but I do know Mum and Dad couldn't be together. The end was inevitable.

While their separation happened instantly, as Mum pulled out of the driveway for the last time, their battle for custody of us kids went on for years. They both wanted full-time custody. At the very least, Dad wanted half and half instead of the one weekend a fortnight he'd initially been given. And so, every now and then, I'd have to go to Family Court and answer questions from a stranger in a suit: 'Are you happy at home? Where do you feel safest? What do you and your brother do with your dad on weekends?'

I don't remember what I would answer – I think I've blanked out those memories – but I used to love to do anything and everything with Dad: going to the beach, bushwalking, camping and even cooking up roadkill on the fire, which was Dad's specialty. Dad would always go on about how he could live off the land and survive in the wild if he had to. 'At least we'd all be okay in an apocalypse,' we'd say.

'Nah, I'd cook you pair up on the barbie first,' he'd joke.

Our weekends with Dad were always happy times. When Dad would pull up out the front of the community centre, we'd race outside to meet him quicker than we could say, 'Bye, Mum!' Dad was a big kid, all lollies and adventures and pranks. He was a friend more than a parent. I'd go to him when I needed a laugh, not when I wanted advice. I had Mum for that.

From the community centre, we'd head straight to the Long Reef boat ramp to visit a stingray we named 'Andre.' Every second Friday, like clockwork, Andre would be waiting for us, and we'd wade out into the water to say g'day to him. Looking back, it was probably a different stingray every time, but that didn't matter. We loved this routine with Dad.

Dad's nature meant Mum was the disciplinarian – she had to be. She was raising two young kids and working full-time as a police officer to put a roof over our heads and food on the table. Mum was – and is – incredible. She's my constant, the person who's always there for me, the one who puts my needs before her own, my emergency contact on every form and the person who always has my back.

Mum is naturally stunning. She's of Greek heritage – quite proudly so – and swears by rubbing olive oil into her golden skin every day. Whether she's ducking down to the corner store to grab a bottle of milk or taking the rubbish bins out, she's always wearing lipstick, statement earrings and a tight belt around her tiny waist. When we were young, she would pick my brother and me up from after-school care looking like she'd just come off the catwalk.

'Why are you dressed up like that?' I'd say, rolling my eyes at her perfectly coordinated outfit.

I definitely inherited my style from my dad, who got around in boardshorts, sarongs and thongs most of the time. I'd get ready in a minute, chucking on a pair of jeans and a t-shirt, and walk out the door without looking in a mirror. I never learned how to straighten or curl my hair, so how it looked when I woke up was how it looked for the rest of the day. When I was a teenager, my mum must have looked at me and thought, 'Where did you come from?'

When I was fourteen, my mum enrolled me and my friend Tiffany in the June Dally-Watkins summer holiday etiquette school. Tiffany wasn't rough around the edges like me, she was much more prim and proper. Every day for a week, Tiffany and I would begrudgingly catch a bus from the Northern Beaches into the city to learn how to sit, walk and eat, and every day for a week, we tried our best to get out of going. Learning how to put make-up on and which cutlery to use during a three-course meal was the last thing we wanted to be doing over the summer. But Mum was so proud of us – especially after the final night's show. All the girls got dressed up in gowns and walked down a catwalk to receive a certificate. I felt ridiculous. Little did I know, there was a model scout in the crowd. You can imagine how chuffed my mum was when I was asked to meet with Vivien's Model Management after the show.

At the meeting the following week, a model agent took my measurements. I hated my height. I was tall and skinny for my age, and I felt self-conscious about it, as teenagers do. I remember trying to slump down to seem shorter and I'm sure the look on my face told the agent I would rather have been anywhere else. I didn't get a call back. But I did go on to do quite a bit of modelling when I got older, and came to love fashion as much as Mum.

I like to think I inherited my mum's talent for sewing, though. Mum made a lot of her clothes, our baby outfits and all of my formal dresses. I'm sure if she wasn't so busy raising a family and working as a cop, she would have got into fashion earlier. That was her passion.

And even though I dressed down most of the time, I loved reading fashion magazines and putting outfits together. My favourite subjects at school (apart from lunch) were Food Tech and Design and Technology. I grew up watching Mum sew and loved doing it at school, except I wasn't very patient and struggled to sit still for a whole lesson.

For me, school wasn't about studying; it was about seeing my mates. I was never an A+ student and had a hard time staying focused. I was the kid rushing to do her homework at her desk the morning it was due because I hadn't done it the night before. I didn't really have career aspirations. I'd always gone with the flow, so I figured I'd keep doing that. I was lost after school, but I didn't mind.

We didn't have much as kids, but we never went without. The stereotype of a Northern Beaches kid is a spoiled brat – we weren't. We didn't have the coolest shoes or brand-spanking-new surfboards or extravagant Christmas trees surrounded by presents, but we did spend school holidays with Dad on a houseboat on the Hawkesbury River. Dave and I always had friends around, too. Whether we were on the houseboat, taking a road trip or going out to dinner, I'd have girlfriends with me. Dad was the fourth or fifth wheel, but he bloody loved it. He was one of us.

When I was an underage teen, before I got my fake ID, Dad would take me and my friends for the Thursday night steak deal at the Mona Vale pub. We'd go to the bistro at 6 pm when it was 'family friendly' time then, when dinner wrapped up, Dad would leave and us girls would go to the bathroom and hide in a cubicle. We'd play cards on the toilet seat (no smart phones then!). Two hours later, after the security guards clocked on and started checking IDs, we'd emerge from the bathroom and into the crowded beer garden where everyone had already been checked for ID. The Mona was famous for its Thursday night DJs – and steaks – so the place was always packed tight like sardines in a can. God it was fun.

Dad only lived down the road, so he'd stay up and wait for us to come home and then listen to us tell him all about our night. He thought our sneaky plan was brilliant. I think he loved being involved, too. It was a fun weekly tradition we had for some time – until the aforementioned fake IDs.

At Christmas, we had another tradition with Dad. Every year, he would say he didn't want any gifts, and every year we pushed for him to name something.

'Oh alright, just get me a stick of surfboard wax then,' he'd say. When he opened his $4 bar of wax, he was always over the moon. Dad was a simple man, and we were a simple family.

I was thick as thieves with my brother, Dave, who was a typical big bro. He used to wrestle with me in the backyard, throw balls at my head and prank me and my friends. It was all done with love – and I'm sure that's why I'm so tough now. I can run into a wall and just keep running, like a boofhead staffy. As much as he gave me a hard time, my brother was super protective. If ever I was in danger, Dave would be there to save the day. As we got older and boys started looking at me differently, he was never far away, making sure I was okay.

I call my brother 'Bro' and my dad 'Dadlet'. Mum is just 'Mum' because she's the boss. Mum is our rock. She is our consistent, calm centre. While Dad was always fun, and living in the moment, Mum was working hard keeping her eye on the bigger picture of caring for us day after day.

Like I said, my childhood was marked by divided lines, but it was also defined by the beach. Most of my memories of growing up have sand in them, and I took every chance I had to be in the ocean. Narrabeen Beach is where I'd hang out with my friends (and where I'd go to sunbake when I wagged school), Freshwater Beach is where my dad taught me to surf and Warriewood Beach is where I said hello to Chumpy that day when we ran into each other on the stairs. Almost every milestone has been marked at a beach.

Even though Chumpy and I were polar opposites in most regards – he chased the snow, I chased the sun; he was a deep thinker, I was a doer; he hugged his parents before bed every night, I said I was tired and went to my room – the beach was always the one thing we had in common.

I love my family and I wouldn't trade them for the world, but we weren't a super close-knit bunch. Coming from a broken home – and not the Brady Bunch kind – things weren't perfect. We certainly weren't sentimental and didn't put much energy or thought into birthdays or Christmas. In fact, we forgot Bro's tenth birthday altogether. We were on a camping holiday in Crescent Head with Dad and some friends, and it got to midday before he piped up that it was his birthday. We rushed into the nearest town, Kempsey, and bought him a cheap stereo and wrapped it in a beach towel. Bro was stoked.

Chumpy's family couldn't have been more different. He'd spend an hour – each – writing Christmas cards for his mum and dad. They were the happiest when it was just the four of them. Chumpy and I came from very different places and very different families.

Growing up, I couldn't wait to leave home and go out into the world on my own. When I met Chumpy, he became my family in one person.

He defined what love looked like. He was my home.

CHAPTER TWO

His Mother's Son – by Chris Pullin

There's a photo of Chumpy from that day. He's eight and his smile takes up his entire face.

It was 1995 and we were on a family holiday in America. Chumpy had just finished his first proper snowboard ride at Heavenly Valley in Lake Tahoe, and he was stoked. We'd been worried that he wouldn't be able to keep up with us on our skis and told him we weren't going to wait for him, but he had proved us wrong and showed a natural talent for snowboarding. That was the day Chumpy became a snowboarder.

At home, we lived at the snow. My wife, Sally, and I ran a ski shop in the Victorian town of Mansfield, and in her teenage years, she represented Australia in cross-country skiing. So it wasn't a shock when our son fell in love with the slopes, but we weren't expecting him to do so on a snowboard. By the time we left the snow fields of Lake Tahoe after four days, Chumpy was already pretty handy on the snowboard. From that moment on, skiing went by the wayside and Chumpy's feet were firmly planted on one board instead.

In those days, snowboarding was a new sport. It certainly wasn't mainstream. Getting a board for a kid was a mission but, luckily, we ran a ski shop, so we were able to track one down. It was called a Hooga Booga and I've still got it.

When he was fourteen, Chumpy took himself over to America to race in the Nor-Am Cup. It was a big trip for a young bloke – and when I say big, I mean freaking huge. We waved Chumpy off at the airport, knowing that when he got on the plane, there was no-one to meet him at the other end. It was a massive gamble for a young bloke, but he was driven and we supported him because we trusted him.

We were deeply criticised for that. People scoffed and said, 'Why are you letting him go? What, do you think he's going to be a champion or something?' We didn't have grand plans of making a champion out of our son, but we did raise him to be his own person.

We might have helped Chumpy get over there, but once he landed in America, he had to find his own way. He made friends on the slopes of a day and couch surfed of a night. One particular night, he slept on a billiard table in a house full of Irishmen. Of course, we worried. Chump was a long way from home. Anything could have happened: he could have broken a leg, got totally lost and ended up in Texas or woken up after a fall with a concussion. He knew no matter what, though, a flight home was just a phone call away. This was before the days of mobile phones, so we racked up huge phone bills on long distance calls over that trip!

Chumpy didn't do very well in terms of winning, but he came home hell-bent on changing that. Step one: sign up for Race Club, a serious training program with professional coaches. It was a big commitment. The club had a reputation for producing Olympians and it really was the training ground for the next generation of winter athletes in Australia. As you would imagine, it was quite an exclusive club for kids – and their parents – to be a part of. The joke goes that while the Race Club dads are working in Melbourne to pay the tuition and screwing their secretaries, the mums are staying at the family ski chalet, shagging the ski instructors.

That wasn't the case for us. We didn't have a lodge on the mountain, and both Sally and I had to work all winter.

In the six months of the ski season, we worked more hours than most people work all year. The shop opened at 6 am and didn't close until after 9 pm. Because of that, we couldn't drop Chumpy off at training every morning, so he would have to catch the bus from Mansfield to Mount Buller – about an hour's trip. On the days when the kids had an early start, he would catch a lift with Bob the snowmaker at 5.30 am. The mornings were early, the days were long and the initial reception from his peers was icy. In a crowd of Melbourne private school kids, Chumpy stood out, with his long hair and public-school accent. He soon won his peers over with his charm and earned their respect by being professional – and winning.

Chumpy competed at the national championships at Falls Creek that same year. He raced in the Alpine event and was gutted to come second. He lost by only a hundredth of a second, but it knocked his confidence, and he was still kicking himself later when we drove to Mount Hotham for the boardercross competition, which wasn't really his strong suit.

I put the hard word on him. 'That's done, Chumpy, the race is over. Don't be thinking about that, let's address what we're going to do tomorrow,' I said. And that's exactly what we did. I spent the night race-prepping Chumpy's board with fluorocarbon wax while he slept.

The next day, Chumpy absolutely smoked it. He was competing against grown men – including a snowboarder named Ben Wordsworth – and he left them in his wake to claim his first big win at the Australian Nationals. Later that afternoon, the Under 16s junior event was on and Chumpy figured he'd enter that too. The kid next to him at the gates looked over and said, 'Aren't you the bloke who just won the Open?' He won the junior event too. At the presentation, though, he was stripped of his cash prize for the Open because he'd raced as a junior in the Under 16s. It was total bullshit, but we couldn't care less. He'd done it, our boy had done it! We drove home to Mansfield with the windows down, the radio up and Chumpy's arms punching the air in victory.

The wins kept on coming, in Australia and overseas. Chumpy's was an underdog story for the ages. Here was a blue-collar kid from the sticks going up against rich kids with ski chalets who were born on the slopes. Not only that – he was an Aussie. At international competitions, they'd often confuse Australia for Austria. After all, Australia was a land of red-dirt and kangaroos, not snowboarders. Well, it was until Chumpy came along and destroyed the stereotype.

In 2007, Chumpy packed up his snowboard and travelled to Austria to compete in the FIS Snowboarding

Junior World Championships, a prestigious event that only happens every two years. He made his way through the heats and qualified for the final. In the race, he was in front to win, with two other riders behind him. Those blokes got tangled up and took out the back of Chumpy's board as they fell. They were able to unscramble themselves and get back on their feet, but Chumpy was down and ended up finishing third. It wasn't gold, but it was a podium finish, and that was enough to get the attention of both the Olympic Winter Institute of Australia and Ski & Snowboard Australia.

When Chumpy got home, the phone rang, inviting us to attend a meeting down in Melbourne with Geoff Lipshut, the Olympic Winter Institute Director. That was how Australia's first professional snowboarding team was formed. Ben Wordsworth – one of the men Chumpy beat in the Mount Hotham race three years earlier – became his coach. Along with fellow snowboarder Damon Hayler, they became a team of three and they travelled the world together, with Chumpy as the athlete, Ben as his coach and Damon as his competition – and his mate. They were all enormously close and had a deep admiration for each other. Geoff, Ben and Damon were pivotal in taking Chumpy from being a fresh-faced kid out on his own to being an athlete on the Australian team.

It's not an exaggeration to say Chumpy was a pioneer in Australian snowboarding. A lot of kids in the sport looked up to him and wanted to be him. One of those kids was Cam Bolton, who was three years younger than Chumpy and idolised him. Chump was his hero, first as his mentor and his teammate, and then as his best mate. The pair travelled the world together, from Veysonnaz in Switzerland to Stoneham outside Quebec City, where Chumpy won the snowboard cross title in 2013. Cam describes Chumpy as a 'relentless' athlete, 'so dominant, intense and ferocious on the slopes,' and also 'incredibly kind and generous to those who are close to him'.

But before he was 'Alex "Chumpy" Pullin, World Champ,' he was his mother's son.

I met Sally in the backseat of a Valiant in 1970. She was thirteen and I was fourteen. We lived in different towns in the Victorian High Country, but we both skied of a weekend and carpooled home together one day after a race. As the story goes, Sally elbowed another girl out of the way to sit next to me. Not that we spoke at all during the drive, but we sat so close our arms 'accidentally' touched. We've been together ever since.

By the mid-eighties, we were in the rhythm of running our ski shop through the winter and sailing for the summer. At the start of 1987, we were planning to sail from the east coast of Australia across the Tasman Sea to New Zealand in our yacht, *Sally Barker*, when Sally started to feel funny. We went to a doctor and, wouldn't you know it, we were pregnant. Holy shit. We were going to have a baby.

We still sailed to New Zealand with Chumpy in Sally's belly: the three of us on our first adventure together. Chumpy inherited his mother's thrill-seeking streak – and her work ethic. Sal worked in the ski shop through the winter, heavily pregnant. The morning before Chumpy was born, she was standing at the counter, giving customers their change and wishing them well on the slopes with her tummy resting on the cash register, as it had been for a number of months. Later that afternoon, Sal went into labour and we went to the hospital to welcome our baby boy: Alex Pullin.

When he was born, the nurse placed Chumpy on Sally's tummy and he lifted his head up and looked at Sally's face. He reached out his tiny, wet and gooey arm and wrapped his fingers around her nipple. He was born strong. Meanwhile, I had to step into the ensuite to wash my face because I was covered in tears. When I came back into the room and saw Sally holding Chumpy in her arms,

I couldn't feel the ground. I wasn't walking, I was floating towards them. The floor beneath me was air. It was the happiest moment of my life.

Chumpy's arrival marked the end of the ski season, so we spent three months at home in our own little bubble. When summer came, we did what we always did and set sail.

We picked up our yacht, *Sally Barker*, from Geelong and sailed it out of the heads of Melbourne, up the East Coast and over to Lord Howe Island. It was Chumpy's first sailing trip earthside, and at the age of six months he'd spent half his life on land and half on water. I remember speaking to a coast operator named Joy Croft on our HF radio. Out at sea, her voice was a calming and reassuring lifeline. When she asked us how many people were on board the yacht, we said two and a half. On cue, Chumpy squawked in the background.

'You have a baby on board?' Joy marvelled.

From that point on, every time we radioed Joy on our yearly trips, she wouldn't ask about the boat or the weather, she'd ask about our boy.

Most babies cry of a morning to let you know they're awake; Chumpy hummed. He'd sing to himself in his cot until I grabbed him and put him in bed with Sal. As a baby, he was very interested in the world. He loved being alive and especially loved feeding time. His chubby rolls gave the Michelin Man a run for his money.

Even though it was the name we gave him, 'Alex' seemed entirely too old for a little boy, so we called him all different nicknames. For a while, he was known as 'Trippin Over' because he fell on his face all the time, but it was 'Chumpy' that stuck. I wish there was some grand story or family tradition behind the name, but it was just a silly nickname. I remember getting report cards from the school for 'Chumpy Pullin', and I can still hear the Eurosport commentator calling the race at the World Cup: 'It's Chumpy leading now, the big Australian who's everybody's friend.'

From the moment they met, Chumpy's best friend was his sister, Emma, who came along when he was three. They were inseparable. As kids, they shared a single bed, knew each other as well as they knew themselves, and could say more with a glance across the table than in an hour's conversation with someone else. Emma never knew a world without Chumpy. He was her world.

We used to do a silly thing at home, where I'd scream out 'Who's your best friend in the world?' and Chumpy would scream back, 'Emmi,' and Emmi would yell, 'Chumpy.' One year, Chumpy addressed Emmi's birthday card to 'My best friend in the world'. In that moment, I knew their relationship superseded everything.

Music was always playing loudly in the house. I'd crank Creedence Clearwater Revival, Talking Heads and Bob Dylan, and Sal would put on Tracy Chapman and Vika and Linda Bull. We had a record player in the lounge room and Chumpy would lie on the carpet next to it, wearing a pair of yellow headphones and listening to tunes, totally oblivious to whatever was going on around him. In the car, we'd sing The Cranberries' classic 'Zombie' driving down the road, though it was more screaming than singing.

Chumpy first picked up a guitar when he was eight. Actually, Sally put the guitar in his lap and taught him how to play it. She played the guitar and sung, while Chumpy strummed and soaked it all in. After a while, Chumpy got better than Sal and we hired a guitar teacher. Chumpy wrote a song about it years later called 'Colour of Your Eyes'.

Here I am playing my mother's old guitar
The notes are thick and sweet like honey from the jar
The way you taught me then is the way that I still
* know*
The memories of us playing together are the ones that
* soothe my soul*

Each afternoon, Chumpy would come home from school and as one arm shrugged off his backpack, the other would reach for his guitar. After dinner, I told the kids they could either do the dishes or play us some songs in the kitchen. It wasn't a hard choice. They'd jam away as we washed the pots and pans and danced along. Chumpy and Emmi learned a song and proudly performed it for us, with Chumpy on the guitar and Em on the 'drums' (a cup, a glass and two pencils). It was a song about Lindsay Lohan, and they thought it was hilarious. And it was.

When Emma turned eight, Chumpy taught her how to play the guitar, just like his mum had done with him. The tradition was held up by the kids. It surpassed us.

The kids had a few different band names over the years: Catchafire, Earthbound and Love Charli. The line-up was Chumpy and Em, with a man named Rolf Koren on percussion. Rolf was a session player who'd worked with a number of bands over the years and was an accomplished musician in his own right. He was forty-five, but he never tried to influence the kids' songs or steer the music in a different direction. He respected Chumpy and Emma and was hugely supportive of their creativity. He never judged or ridiculed them, and always made them feel comfortable trying out new sounds and throwing around lyrics. Rolf wasn't just their percussionist, he became their friend and confidant. He gave the band a certain credibility; they weren't just kids mucking around, they were the real deal.

The kids weren't too keen on the name Rolf, though, so they nicknamed him Zigi. It was a band of nicknames: Chumpy, Zigi and Cinque, which is the name Emma went by for a while. During that time, she wore a tasseled hat (that was actually a lampshade) on her head at gigs. She also played a beautiful bass guitar, which she named the Black Pearl long before *Pirates of the Caribbean* existed.

I remember a particularly great Love Charli gig at The Produce Store in Mansfield. The joint was packed to the rafters so the crowd spilled onto the footpath outside. That's where Sally and I watched the show. It was a summer's day and the music wafted down the street, drawing more people to the gig. The kids were going off and the crowd was loving it! It was so busy, Sal bumped into the bloke behind her. 'Oh sorry,' she apologised.

'No worries. You've got some really talented kids there,' he said.

'Thanks,' she replied, looking him up and down. 'I feel like I know you, do I?'

'Nah, we've never met,' said the man, who was Nathan Buckley, a big-shot AFL player.

Sal must have been the only person in the footy-obsessed town of Mansfield who didn't know who Buckley was. He was on TV at least three times a week and was quite the legend around our parts.

As well as counting Nathan Buckley as a fan, Love Charli had a decent following around town, and they were booked to play paid gigs and festivals. The kids were still teenagers when they recorded their own album. On the CD, they listed the music studio as Amber Studios.

'Where the hell is Amber Studios?' I asked them with a raised eyebrow.

'Downstairs,' they said, nodding to the ground level of the ski shop where we lived. 'We thought Amber Studios sounded cooler.'

Between music, snowboarding and sailing, there wasn't a lot of time for much else. At high school, Chumpy was popular in that people enjoyed his company – especially the girls – but I think he felt like a fish out of water. For one, he didn't play football or cricket, which wasn't ideal at a ball-crazed school.

One day, Chumpy came home from school upset. 'I just haven't got any friends,' he said. 'All the guys are playing footy and going to parties on the weekend, then spending the rest of the week talking about what happened at the last party and what's going to happen at the next one.'

It wasn't as though Chumpy wasn't invited to these parties – he was – but he was preoccupied with the snow and the songs and the sea. And our family, which was his world. Why would Chumpy want to go to a party when he could be at home with us and his sister?

Emmi was by his side in all the elements. When it came to his music, Chumpy looked to his sister for her nod of approval. Emma was as sharp as a diamond; if she didn't like something, her disapproval cut deep, but when she did approve, her rubber stamp made things shine. Chumpy sought out that stamp and basked in its glow when he got it.

The feeling was mutual. Emma had written a song called 'The One' that sounded like she was describing her soulmate, but she was actually singing about a much-wanted Kombi van. She was going to perform the song for the first time at a pub in Mount Buller and she was absolutely shitting herself. Mind you, she was fourteen. When she started singing – with Chumpy on stage beside her, playing the guitar – her voice quivered. She was collapsing and Chumpy knew it, but as much as he wanted to catch her, he couldn't step in and sing for her. Instead, when the chorus came, he did an intense guitar riff. He really beefed it up and put his soul into it. He made sure Emma could hear it and she got his message loud and clear: he was there for her, right beside her, cheering her on.

Back then, smoking was still allowed in pubs, so Chump and Em left the place smelling like an ashtray and croaking with raspy voices. They were beaming, walking down the street to the car. Sal and I were their pseudo-roadies, so we were carrying their gear while they laughed together, arm in arm, basking in the afterglow of the gig. I swear, they both grew an inch, they were walking so tall.

When I close my eyes and picture Chumpy and Emmi together, I see them on our sailing boat, *Southpaw*, in New Caledonia. That boat was loosely named after Chumpy, who was left-handed and would've been a southpaw if he'd been a boxer. Chumpy and Em were aged ten and seven when we sailed *Southpaw*, all sun-kissed skin, salty hair and cheesy smiles. This was their natural element: out on the water, together, arms wrapped around each other.

When we were anchored out on the lagoon, we woke up to splashes and squeals of joy, the sounds of two kids jumping into the water. If I could bottle that sound and listen to it like a shell from the sea, I would.

I know it sounds like an idyllic childhood – and most of the time it was – but we certainly had our moments as well. I remember Chumpy's first week of primary school. He came home one day and pushed Em in the chest, knocking her over. I sat him down and gave him the hard word. 'That isn't going to fly. We don't do that. Whatever happened at school, or whatever's going to happen, that's not how we act,' I said after Chumpy admitted a kid had pushed him over at school and he explained that he'd just done the same.

We didn't have many harsh words between us, but I remember the ones we did clearly. After an overseas snowboarding trip, Chumpy came home with a big head. I mean, he was a talented snowboarder, sure, but he didn't have a score on the board yet. Our small town of Mansfield was home to a very successful cyclist named Simon Gerrans, who won a stage of the Tour de France, among other things. He was doing a motivational speech at the school auditorium and, at the last minute, Chumpy decided he didn't want to go. He must've thought he knew it all. What could he learn from a champion athlete that he didn't already know? Well, Chumpy missed out because it was a really great – and honest – talk. I told him as much when we got home. I said it was piss-weak that he didn't come along.

Later, Chumpy came out of his bedroom with his head hung low and apologised. 'I'm sorry, Dad. I should have been there,' he said, and then we spoke about what we'd do next time.

Our kids' biggest fear was disappointing us. All it took was a slight shake of my head for them to know that they'd done the wrong thing, and they'd bend over backwards to make it right.

Sal and I raised our kids with love, but we never blew smoke up their arses. If they lost a race, we wouldn't tell them we were proud of them because they did their best. We'd say, 'Well, I know you tried, but that was pretty hopeless.' In the same way, when our kids did something outstanding, we'd be honest about it. When Chumpy won his first World Championship in 2011 – which made him Australia's first ever snowboarding world champ – I sent him a message, quoting our favourite line from the film *Babe*: 'That'll do, Chump; that'll do.'

When people ask me what I'm most proud of about Chumpy, it's not the World Championship trophies, the sponsorship deals or industry awards that come to mind: it's the way he made people feel. Chumpy was an extremely talented individual, but he was also just a lovely human being. When he had a conversation with someone, he made them feel like they were the only person in the room. I've had more than one person tell me about brief encounters they had with Chumpy, and how those meetings changed their lives. One of our mantras was, 'The brave and the generous have the best lives because they are seldom sorry.'

Chumpy was brave and generous. It kills me to write that sentence in past tense. *He was*.

I should be writing *is* – Chumpy *is* brave and generous. He is his sister's best friend. And he is his mother's son.

CHAPTER THREE

Falling

Chumpy and I had a New Year's Day tradition. It started back in 2013 after our first New Year's Eve together. We trekked up to Barrenjoey Lighthouse, overlooking Palm Beach on Sydney's Northern Beaches, with a bottle of champagne, snacks, a picnic blanket and Chumpy's guitar. We found a flat rock on the edge of the cliff with the most epic views of the coast, and it became 'our rock.' I sat behind Chumpy and wrapped my legs around his waist, like a little koala cuddling a eucalyptus tree. Chumpy strummed his guitar and I looked out to the water with my head resting on his shoulder.

In that moment, it felt like we were the only people in the world. And that's exactly the way we liked it.

It became a ritual. Every New Year's Day, we'd head to our rock and make our resolutions for the year ahead. Most years, I'd resolve to drink less alcohol and eat less sugar – while sipping champagne and snacking on chocolate. Chumpy's resolutions were always more poignant. 'I don't want to change a thing because this is too good. My resolution is for everything to stay exactly the same,' he said once.

Things had been perfect that first New Year's Day. Chumpy was ending 2012 on a high after doing well in the first stages of the FIS Snowboarding World Cup. When he got back from overseas, he spent Christmas with his family in Eden, and his sister later told me he was giddy like a puppy to see me.

Chumpy came to stay with me for a week at Mum's house in Narrabeen. Mum was looking forward to meeting the dream boy I'd been talking to nonstop. It wasn't until Mum googled Chumpy that I started to realise he was *somebody*. I didn't follow snow sports, so I had no idea he'd been to the Olympics and was a World Champion. Mum watched videos of Chumpy competing and giving interviews and was impressed. Then he made us his family's famous spaghetti bolognese for dinner and she was totally dazzled. So was I.

I felt like such a kid around Chump. He was so worldly and wise, and I was as carefree as they come. We might have been on different wavelengths, but Chumpy must have seen some promise in me. He made me want to grow up and meet him on his level. In a way, we grew up together and he moulded the woman I became.

We spent most of that week together at the beach, swimming in the surf, lazing on the sand, soaking up the sun and kissing each other's salty lips. After a morning at the beach, I was in the shower with Chumpy when he first told me he loved me. It had been on the tip of both of our tongues, but he was the first one to say it out loud. I could tell he'd been bursting to, but was waiting for the right moment, which happened to be when we were rinsing the salt and sand off each other. We were staring at each other and I knew we were thinking the same thing. I'd started falling in love with him on the dance floor two months before, and fell deeper with every message exchanged from afar, but spending those sticky summer days together pushed me over the edge entirely.

Of course, I told him I loved him straight back. I'd never been surer of anything in my life. We were solid. We didn't have an explicit conversation about being official or becoming boyfriend/girlfriend. We didn't need to. We just *were*.

Unlike my previous relationships, I didn't have to worry about Chumpy being faithful or trustworthy. He was so committed to me and our relationship. He told me he was in it for the long haul and he wanted to look after me, no matter what. There was no bullshit, no empty promises and no wondering if the grass was greener on the other side of the fence. Our grass was as green as it could get.

There's a photo of Chumpy as a toddler wearing a blue t-shirt with 'Chumpy' written in white block letters. The story I heard before I got to know Chumpy was that his parents nicknamed him 'Champion', which morphed into 'Champ' and then somehow became 'Chumpy' – and the rest is history. It fits him so perfectly. I called him Alex when we first got together because I thought Chumpy was a nickname only his mates used, but when I heard his mum call him Chumpy and saw her confused expression when I referred to him as Alex, I dropped the formalities. I called him Chumpy, Bear or Bluey, and he called me Elmo, El Loco or Bub, usually Bub.

When Chumpy introduced me to his parents, I'm sure they were thinking, 'Who the hell is this random surfy chick from the Northern Beaches who doesn't know a thing about snowboarding?' I was quite the departure from Chumpy's previous girlfriend, a professional snowboarder from Bulgaria. I didn't even know there was a difference between boardercross and halfpipe snowboarding (Chumpy did the former, I soon learned).

His parents might have been put off by my lack of fawning interest in Chumpy's sport, but they came to see that as a positive. I was happy-go-lucky and that rubbed off on Chump. I brought out his silly, cheeky side and I think he needed that. I gave him permission to be himself – a total dork.

Emma used to say we were the definition of 'opposites attract'. I was the yin to his yang. Chumpy was a classic Virgo; a perfectionist neat freak who kept his car spotless. Meanwhile, I was 'rough-and-tumble' – as Em describes me – and would jump straight into the passenger seat, feet still sandy from the beach. 'Some of the beach is coming home with us,' I'd joke when I saw Chumpy's face twitch at the mess.

When Chumpy was competing and training, he was so dedicated, hardworking and serious. Before every race, he'd listen to the *Vikings* theme song to get in the zone and channel his inner Ragnar Lothbrok. In that moment, he wasn't a snowboarder; he was a Viking ready for battle.

The Viking obsession wasn't limited to the slopes. Chumpy's dad found an old axe in the bush near their house after a fire and he restored it, adding a carved wooden handle. Chumpy saw the axe on a trip home and wanted to make his own, so they did it together in the shed. Then Chumpy got a picture of an axe tattooed on his ribs, with the motto 'all in' written in Viking runes. That was the way Chumpy lived his life: he went all in. He didn't half-arse anything. That was certainly the case when it came to our relationship: from day one, he was all in.

During our first year together, I celebrated my twenty-first birthday on a girls' trip to the States. A group of my friends and I travelled from San Diego to San Francisco and ended up in Las Vegas for my birthday. I was sitting in my hotel room in Sin City with my closest girlfriends when Chumpy's birthday present for me arrived.

It was a song.

In the email, he wrote, 'I want to send this to you, El. It's nothing amazing at all, it just kind of came together. I'm not a songwriter. I'm not a musician. But here's a song for you from me.'

He was full of shit – very humble, modest shit – because he was a natural muso. Chumpy told me to listen to the song with headphones on because it was personal. Of course,

I turned the speaker up high and blasted it for everyone to hear. We jumped around screaming and dancing. The song was called 'Falling', and the chorus made me cry.

I've got the strongest feeling, my love has found its home in your heart.
'Cos baby, I'm falling like I had no warning, but it feels so good.

God, it felt so good!

Chumpy organised to meet me in Hawaii after my girls' trip, to continue the celebrations. We met at Honolulu airport. I saw him before he saw me. Chumpy was standing at the counter of the car hire shop, and I stopped for a moment to drink in the sight of him. His hair had grown but his skin was as golden as ever.

When we jumped in the hire car and hit the road to our beach house on the north shore, we couldn't stop screaming and smiling. We were in Hawaii! Together! At last!

Our time in Hawaii was the definition of the honeymoon period. We were obsessed with each other. Our hands were never not touching, and our eyes were never not locked. We couldn't get physically close enough to each other; even when I was sitting in his lap with his arms wrapped all the way around my waist, I wanted to be closer.

Our days were a holiday haze of lying on the beach, eating ice-cream and being tangled up in bed. In between the sheets, we talked about our future and mapped out our life together. Chumpy didn't say things for the sake of saying them, he meant every word he said and thought through every decision he made. So when he asked me to move in with him when we got back home to Sydney, I knew it was the real deal. And I knew we were going to have the best fucking time together. I could see where our lives were going, and I sure liked the view.

Those two weeks in Hawaii were some of the happiest of our lives. Chumpy was in a really good place in his career and had taken out the boardercross World Champion title for the second time. World champs are presented with a crystal globe trophy and Chumpy was one of the few people in the world to have two of them! Not that Chumpy was in the sport for the bling, but they were a testament to his ridiculous talent and hard work.

Chumpy was stoked with all the success he was having, and I was stoked for him, but there was another reason we couldn't stop smiling: we'd found each other. I couldn't believe I'd fallen in love with the best person in the world and that he loved me back. I had to keep touching Chumpy to make sure he was real. And because I liked touching him!

When we returned from Hawaii, the honeymoon period just kept on rolling. We moved in together straightaway. It was Chumpy's idea and I was totally on board.

I didn't grow up believing in true love, but Chumpy was making a believer out of me.

CHAPTER FOUR

All In

For a bloke who grew up sailing different seas every summer and spent half his adult life travelling to far-flung ski slopes, Chumpy was quite the homebody. He was so proud when he bought his first apartment, in Dee Why on Sydney's Northern Beaches. He'd been wanting to move to the area permanently for some time instead of being based at his parents' place, and finally found the perfect two-bedroom apartment. It was a modern place overlooking a park and a short walk to the beach. It was never just 'Chumpy's' apartment; he was adamant that it was 'ours', and after we got back from Hawaii, we picked out some colourful stools, bought the world's comfiest couch and made it our home.

We'd been living together for a few months when Chumpy opened up a joint bank account for us. It's not something I asked for – especially knowing I couldn't contribute as much as him – but he insisted. He wanted to share every part of his life with me. It was unlike any relationship I'd been in – or seen growing up. After my mum left my dad, he swore off marriage for good and became a lifelong bachelor. He warned my brother about getting married and told us both to look after ourselves first. You can't lose everything if you never give it away.

Chumpy was the complete opposite. He was committed and open-hearted. He was all in, and so was I.

Life fell into a nice little routine. Every morning, we'd walk down to Dee Why Beach to check out the surf and grab a coffee at the same café, Sea Bar. As a special treat, we'd share a slice of banana bread with extra butter. In the early days, I was studying for a business degree, so I'd head to university and Chumpy would go to the gym to train. When I started working an office job in Freshwater, Chumpy would meet me every day for lunch. On a good day, we'd squeeze in a swim at the beach together. There were a lot of good days.

Even the hard days were good with Chumpy. In 2014, I had routine eye surgery to remove a pterygium that was growing on my eye. Somehow, he made that whole procedure and hospital stay an enjoyable experience. Chumpy snapped a photo of me looking 'glam' in my hospital gown and joked that they had to give me a double shot of sleeping juice to knock me out because I was so excited about the outfit. We were always joking, laughing, taking the piss out of each other. Chumpy had a habit of putting on random accents and doing impromptu impressions. We'd be out to dinner and he'd order in a thick Kiwi accent and I'd be in stitches. Maybe you had to be there.

Chump was a talker, especially at night when I was half-asleep. He'd call his chats 'scuba diving' because he was never surface-level chatting, it was always *very* important and deep. Meanwhile, I was a sleeper. Chumpy knew that as soon as my head hit the pillow, I was out and my ears were off, but he'd try to keep me awake.

'Can you just email me the rest of the story?' I'd jokingly say in response, quoting one of our favourite movies, *Ted*. He was so deep, and I could be flippant. That was a blessing and a curse.

We didn't fight. This isn't me looking back with rose-coloured glasses. I can only remember having one serious argument with Chumpy in our entire eight-year relationship. I can't even remember what it was over – it might have even been something as small as a miscommunication about what we were having for dinner – but for some reason, we were pissed off with each other. I'm the kind of person who can shrug that off and wake up in the morning with a clean slate, but Chumpy needed to talk any issue through before he could go to bed. And so we stayed up until 2 am, talking about this minuscule issue. I was so tired, but Chumpy was adamant we had to get to the bottom of it and make sure we were completely, one hundred per cent fine. Finally, in the early hours of the morning, we cuddled up together and fell asleep. And then we started the next day with a clean slate. Funny that.

In an interview we did with the website *Buro 24/7* while we were living in Sydney, Chumpy said it perfectly: 'For me personally, with El, it's really nice to be able to break things down and focus on the simple things. Doing what I do it's really easy to get caught up in trying to hone in on every detail,' he explained. 'I probably overprepare, whereas El's totally the opposite. For instance, we'll play mini golf. I'll walk up, look at the hole, put my ball in where I think. She drops the ball, and practically hits it while it's still bouncing, and she'll sink the hole in one. I'll probably get close, but sometimes thinking is the enemy. Just let it be.'

When the journalist asked Chumpy his favourite quality of mine, he said, 'Just that she's happy all the time. It doesn't matter what's going on, her ability to just wake up, smile, laugh, have a good time ... it's her energy. It just boils away inside of her. El wakes up happy, so it really puts me in a good place.'

Chumpy was away so often, competing on the snowboarding circuit, that it made us cherish our time together even more. When he was with me in Sydney, we didn't waste a second. And when he was away overseas, we counted down the seconds. We'd hug and cry at the airport every time he left, but I didn't fret for him. I enjoyed the independence and the butterflies I felt when I got a message from him or knew he was coming home soon. There was something exciting about that anticipation. Picking him up from the airport was the best feeling in the world. I always picked him up even though he could have easily got in a taxi. We were that nauseating couple at the arrivals gate, running in to each other's arms and kissing, even if he'd only been away for a couple of weeks.

When Chumpy was away – and even when he was home – I spent most of my time working. I've always been a worker. Straight after high school, I went to TAFE to do an endorsed enrolled nursing diploma. It was a year-long course – including 700 hours of practical work – that prepared people to go to university to become a registered nurse. I undertook my 700-hour placement at a psychiatric hospital in Sydney, where I worked in the eating disorder ward with patients who had anorexia and bulimia, and on the mood disorder ward with people experiencing depression, PTSD and bipolar disorder. It was an eye-opening experience. At breakfast in the eating disorder ward, the patients would look at me like I was an alien for putting butter on my toast and following it with cereal. Meanwhile, they were trying to sneakily scrape the butter off their own toast under the table to avoid eating it.

I still have the faces of some of the patients etched in my brain. I saw grown men trembling with fear, unable to speak because their trauma was too big and dark to say out loud. My time sitting in on therapy sessions at the hospital shaped my worldview. Mental illness doesn't discriminate. It affects people from all backgrounds, regardless of wealth, social standing or education. So many people have shit going on in their life and noise in their mind – and you wouldn't necessarily know it from looking at them.

I learned so much from my stint at the hospital, but it was gnarly. I was eighteen, just out of school, and working with very unwell people. It felt like too much responsibility for someone that age. Most nursing students go to university after high school so they don't do their practical work until the end of their three-year degree when they're twenty-one. If I had been older, I might have pursued nursing further – it's such an interesting field – but I was totally out of my depth and so while I got my diploma, I didn't go on to do nursing at university as I'd planned. Still, that year taught me so much. It made me realise that there's always someone worse off.

Before I started my nursing diploma, while I was still in high school, I worked at the local nursing home on weekends, and I kept doing so into my early twenties. It was always my job on the side, and I stayed there for so long because 1) it was great money and 2) heaps of my friends worked there. Plus, helping to care for the patients, making tea and cooking food for them was pretty easy work. I'd been there for years when my dad's mum, my Oma, moved in as a resident. It was quite weird for me, and I struggled to work there after her arrival. During my shifts, I always wanted to just go and visit her instead of working. And a lot of times I did! I'd sneak off to her room and spend a few hours hanging out with her when I was meant to be on the clock. Oma was so cute, and she was incredibly close to my dad. Every time her phone rang when I was with her, she'd answer it by saying, 'Petey boy!' And every time it wasn't Dad, she'd be so disappointed. Oma lasted a few years at the nursing home before she died of old age. Getting to spend extra time with her that I might not have had if I didn't work at the nursing home was a blessing.

I had a lot of different jobs over the years, but I didn't really have a career – not in the same way Chumpy did, anyway.

I didn't often get a chance to travel with Chumpy when he competed, but that suited me fine. I don't think I was cut out for the WAG life, and I hate the cold. So the first time I got to see Chumpy compete on a grand scale overseas was at the 2014 Sochi Winter Olympics. Before I left Sydney, I spread banners out on the floor at home and painted, 'We Love U Chumpy – Bring Home The Gold.'

Chumpy didn't buy into the hype of the Olympics. Of course, he recognised their significance and felt a sense of pride representing his country, but the Olympics were a single competition that happened every four years, whereas the World Championships spanned the snow season each year and were the real barometer of the sport's best. Also, the Olympics were often more about bureaucracy, sponsorship money and egos.

Going into Sochi, Chumpy was apprehensive. For one, the only restaurant at the Olympic Village for the athletes was McDonald's (who happened to be a sponsor of the event). And for two, he knew the conditions on the course weren't going to be great because they were using artificial snow, which is entirely different from the real thing and not at all ideal for competing. The pressure was on, the tension was high, and the people were ... difficult.

I was in Venice with my mum, on my way over to Russia for the Games, when Australia's opening ceremony flagbearer was announced at a press conference. We were at an old pub watching the news coverage on the TV. 'I have asked the person who I think truly represents this generation of Australian winter sports to carry the flag at the opening ceremony tomorrow night, the Australian athlete who has had the Australian flag flying more often and higher across the world stage over the last four years since Vancouver and the man that embodies the spirit and drive of this team,' said Ian Chesterman, the Chef de Mission of the Australian team. 'Ladies and gentlemen, it gives me great pleasure to announce that the flagbearer for the 2014 Olympic team is Alex Pullin.'

It was hard to hear Chumpy's speech over our squeals of excitement, but his smile said it all. He was chuffed. 'Wow, this is an amazing honour,' I managed to hear him say after skier Lydia Lassila passed him the flag. 'I'm going to wave this flag really proud.'

When I arrived in Sochi, the energy wasn't quite as joyous.

It was dark and cold, and the morning of Chumpy's event was marred by a media storm when, in an open letter emailed to journalists the day before, Bruce Brockhoff (of the Brockhoff Biscuit dynasty and father of fellow Australian snowboarder Belle Brockhoff) levelled his frustrations with the Australian Olympic Committee about his daughter's funding at Chumpy. Bruce was upset that his daughter wasn't getting as much funding as what he believed Chumpy was, who received the support he did because of the success he'd had. When the funding was allocated, Chumpy was the only Australian World Championship snowboard cross competitor.

News reports quoted Mr Brockhoff as saying that if Chumpy failed to deliver there would be dozens of Aussies in the know 'dancing on the graves' of Olympic officials. It was a brutal comment and I knew it hurt Chumpy, but I didn't realise just how much it affected him until much later. On the morning of his event, Chumpy woke up dry-retching and vomiting in the bathroom basin. The debate around the email was incredibly stressful, and that stress was magnified by the fact he was meant to compete that day. Chumpy played it off like it was no big deal and put on a brave face, but underneath it all, he was gutted.

For better or worse, Chumpy's event ended up being postponed for a day due to fog. Somehow Chumpy managed to switch off the bullshit in his mind and he did really well in the first heat, but sadly crashed out in the quarterfinals. It was tough. He'd been the country's best hopes of a gold medal, but he finished in unlucky equal 13th place. Chumpy immediately went into analysis mode and replayed his run over and over again so he could pinpoint the moment it went wrong and do better next time.

The fallout was as tough as the loss itself. On the back of Bruce's letter, the media flamed gossip stories of team rivalries and questioned if the Australian Olympic Committee's investment in Chumpy was 'worth it'.

It's a misconception that Olympic athletes are paid a stack of taxpayer money. When it was reported that Chumpy received $500,000 in funding, not everyone realised that was over four years and it wasn't cash; it was 'program operations', meaning the money paid for his coach, physiotherapy and other training expenses. Athletes only receive prize money if they win, and Chumpy earned his living through his hard work on sponsorships deals.

During the controversy, the Olympic Winter Institute of Australia stayed silent. We knew they would have been trying to be apolitical and wanting to avoid stoking the fire, but it was a silence that impacted on Chumpy. He was their flagbearer and had given his all to that Olympic team. He'd always had a warm and friendly relationship with the Institute. That warmth cooled in Sochi. He was still an absolute professional and a fierce athlete, but something changed in him. He saw the Institute for what they were – an organisation.

Bruce ended up issuing an apology for his comments. 'I apologise to all those who feel they have been offended, including family. It was never my intention to upset the men's boardercross event nor any of the contestants, especially Alex "Chumpy" Pullin, Jarryd Hughes nor Cameron Bolton on the Australian Olympic team,' Bruce said.

As usual, Chumpy took the high road. 'It was sad to see there was a negative spike to all the positivity around the Winter Olympics, certainly, but for me, my personal approach in Russia was to focus on the track. And I definitely needed all that focus because the conditions thrown at us were tough,' said Chumpy. 'I am happy with my performance there. I put everything on the line, but unfortunately, it didn't go my way.'

I was proud of Chumpy for the four years of training he put in, his effort on the track (despite the crap conditions), and his grace under pressure. Like everyone, Chumpy didn't enjoy losing. He struggled with failure, and spent a lot of time going over his mistakes to make some kind of peace with them. He'd write lists of learnings, notes for what to do next time and self-talk suggestions, including 'There's no place I'd rather be' and 'I'm ready'.

Eventually, he'd cop it on the chin, but it took some processing. What's that inspirational quote? 'It's not about how many times you fall down. It's about how many times you get back up.' Chumpy always got back up, and he didn't just bounce back, he dominated, finishing second on the World Cup standings after a ripper 2014/2015 season.

One of Chumpy's favourite places to snowboard was Austria and when I joined him on a trip there, I could see why. We stayed at a ski resort called Hintertux Gletscher and I couldn't get over the beauty of the place. Our room had a view of the snow-capped mountains, and it was like something out of a fairytale or a postcard or a winter wonderland snow globe. We spent our days on the slopes and our nights by the fire, eating schnitzel and drinking red wine with Chump's coach, Ben Wordsworth, and his lovely wife Edwina. Because Chumpy stayed there every year with the Australian team for the World Cup event, he knew the owners of the hotel quite well. They loved him. Chumpy would bring his guitar and do live shows for the guests after dinner. It became an institution of sorts, and some guests would book their holiday based on when

Chumpy would be there. The energy was something else, and Chumpy was well and truly in his element.

In 2015, Chumpy somehow managed to have an entire month off, so we jumped on a plane and met his parents in New Caledonia to join them on their boat, *Sea Whiskers*. Just the four of us for four weeks, living on top of each other out at sea, completely off the grid, with no internet connection. Did I mention I get really bad seasickness?

When I told my mates I was doing a sailing trip with my in-laws, they thought I was mad. And I might well have been, but I have some great memories from that month together. That trip was when I really became a part of the family, that I really understood who Chris and Sal were, and that they got to know me. They also got to see me and Chumpy together as a couple, and how blissfully happy we made each other.

It was all hands on deck. They were all master sailors and worked together like a well-oiled machine. They communicated in nods, grunts and raised eyebrows. While they were reading the wind and adjusting the sails, I was down in the kitchen, whipping up snacks. We sailed around the Loyalty Islands and there were some days we didn't see land. I popped seasickness tablets the entire time.

Every day on the boat was a sunny blur of colourful coral, fresh fish on the barbeque, sunset rums and guitar strumming. It gave me such an insight into what Chumpy's childhood would have been like, and a lot of respect for the unconventional way his parents raised him.

I remember one particular day on *Sea Whiskers* when we all came down with a serious case of cabin fever. We put on some wacky music and danced around like lunatics until we were bent over with laughter. It was a special time – not many adults can take a month out of their lives to sail around with their parents or in-laws. We never wanted to leave.

When Chumpy and I had to head back to Australia, our goodbyes stretched on like the horizon that had been guiding us for four weeks. There were hugs and tears and more hugs. Chumpy and I left *Sea Whiskers* to head to a tiny island airport to catch our flight to New Caledonia and then transit on to Sydney. The local airport was more like a school canteen, and when we arrived, after an hour's drive from the coast, we found out our flight had been cancelled due to bad weather.

Not to worry, I said. We get another night on the boat. Great. But first we had to get there …

Chumpy and I hitchhiked from the airport back to the beach where the boat was moored and were glad to see it was still there. Standing on the sand with all of our luggage piled up next to us, we could see *Sea Whiskers*, but Chris and Sal couldn't see us. We waved our arms and shouted until our voices gave out, but they couldn't hear us over the wind.

Then it got dark – really dark. We contemplated sleeping on the beach, but gave it one more crack. Under the moonlight, Chumpy 'borrowed' a canoe from the beach and started to paddle out to the boat. By this time, the wind was roaring and the current was strong. I could barely see Chumpy in the darkness, and the five minutes it took him to paddle out felt like forever. I was seriously scared that he might get swept out to sea and wouldn't come back, but all I could do was dig my feet into the sand and hope for the best. I knew he'd made it when the boat's lights came on and I spotted the dinghy coming over to the beach to pick me up. Hallelujah!

We spent another rum-tipsy night together and repeated our farewells the next day. Chumpy's parents named the boat *Sea Whiskers* after one of his songs and the lyrics summed up the trip nicely:

You know as soon as we reach the port that we're
   bound for
Cheers to a great life and what else could we ask for

As beautiful as it is to have the memories of our sailing trip, it blows my mind to think that from that moment, we'd only have five more years with Chumpy. There should have been so many more trips, so many more rum-fuelled cabin fever dance parties and so, so many more family hugs.

CHAPTER FIVE

Two of Us

I used to lovingly tease Chumpy about keeping a diary. He'd carry a notebook around with him and write to himself about life and work, his fears and hopes. He'd also make performance notes after each competition and scribble down song lyric ideas in the moment.

As much as I joked about the diaries at the time, I'm now ridiculously grateful for them. The sight of Chumpy's handwriting makes my heart swell, and his entries take me right back to the moments we shared. I know part of him will cringe at the thought of me reading his unfinished lyrics and random musings, but he'd also know how much those thoughts mean to me now. In 2016, he wrote:

I'm packing up about to leave for Germany World Championships. Chrissy was so good with family and summer. Elle and me are amazing, although she is in Central America now. I'm feeling good, but a bit lonely at home without her and I'm missing the action. I just wanna race!

I love my home with Elle. I love my life, but I gotta get out and go fast for the next few months. I'm fit, mentally in a good place, all that's left to do is just go out and do it!

He also wrote:

Just a quick note to mention that while I was waiting in the lounge in Sydney airport, one of the actors from Vikings – Ragnar's second missus – walked in. Ha! I reckon that's got to be a good omen.

It was. When he got to Germany, Chumpy placed third at the World Cup competition there and went on to win gold at Baqueira Beret in Spain at the final World Cup event of the season. At the same event, his Aussie teammate Belle Brockhoff took out the women's title – the first time Australia won gold in the women's and men's events at a major competition. It was a milestone in the sport.

While Chumpy was marking milestones, I was back at home in Dee Why doing what I always did: working.

And partying. And working again. As well as the nursing home and my office job in Freshwater during that time, I also worked at a nice dress shop in Manly and did some modelling jobs on the side too. I've always been go-go-go. Back in the day, I would go out to the Newport pub at night and back it up with work in the morning, or get drunk at a house party and wake up early to go to the gym. It was a classic case of being young and able to bounce back after a big night. There was plenty of bouncing back during our years in Dee Why. We lived a lot of life there. It felt like we were always doing something, having mates over for cocktails, going on adventures in the bush, celebrating engagements, weddings, babies and birthdays. That didn't stop when Chumpy was away.

The year 2017 marked another milestone: Chumpy's thirtieth birthday. We went all out and rented a house at Boomerang Beach on the mid-north coast of New South Wales for a long weekend away with all of our friends. It was well and truly spring and the weather turned it on for us. For three days, we hit the surf, cracked the beers and cranked the barbeque for epic cook-ups every night. I have this distinct memory of dancing under the stars with Chump, surrounded by our favourite people and feeling so content. Chumpy said it was his best birthday yet. Months later, when our friends gathered again to celebrate New

Year's Eve, we all went around in a circle to share our highs and lows of the year that was. Almost everyone listed Chump's thirtieth as their favourite moment of the year.

Chumpy and I had two highlights – that weekend, and moving to the Gold Coast.

At thirty, Chumpy wanted to put down roots. After five happy years in Dee Why, we had dreams of moving out of Sydney and buying a house together. As much as Chumpy loved his parent's home in Eden and where I grew up on the Northern Beaches, he always wanted to find a place we could grow together, as a couple and a family. We found that place on the Gold Coast.

The southern beaches of the Gold Coast are almost like a sister city to the Northern Beaches in Sydney. A lot of our mates had made the move to Queensland, so we'd spent a fair bit of time there over the years visiting them. Chumpy and I booked a trip to the Goldy in 2017 to inspect places, mostly rundown shacks that needed major work. We had a break in our showing schedule and decided to head along to a viewing of a place we thought was way out of our reach. The house was on top of a hill, a suburb back from the sea, with distant views of Palm Beach. On the real estate website, it looked fake, too perfect – the grass was fluorescent green, the pool sparkled and the ceilings were sky-high, like a goddamn display home.

Chumpy's dad, Chris, and mum, Sally, will tell you they called him all different nicknames when he was a baby, but it was 'Chumpy' that stuck. From the moment they met, Chumpy's best friend was his sister, Emma, who came along when he was three. Chumpy loved the snow and the sea and his family.

My family. Bro (Dave), Mum (Karen), Dad (Pete). I love them all the same, but I can't even imagine a world where Mum and Dad are in it together. I've seen them talk to each other probably twice in my entire life. One of those times was at Chumpy's funeral. They couldn't be more opposite. Mum's my foundation. My rock. She's the very reason I keep going – she taught me survival skills and how to keep my head above water when I feel like I'm drowning. Dad is where I get my free spirit and carefree energy from and the person I turn to when I need a laugh (and the best bear hug in the world). Bro is my best friend – he's my person now, I feel him right by my side even when we're apart. He's my and Minnie's everything!

Chumpy's cover of Bon Iver's 'Skinny Love' was my favourite. If Chump wasn't a snowboarder, there's no doubt he would've been a musician. The Pullin home was always full of music. Sally's guitar became Chumpy's. Every day, he and Emma would play it and make up songs together. Chumpy always had a guitar close!

In 1995, Chris, Sal, Chumpy and Emma were on a family holiday in America. Chumpy had just finished his first proper snowboard ride at Heavenly Valley in Lake Tahoe, and he was stoked. That was the day Chumpy became a snowboarder. It was the start of his epic adventures and he'd go on to become a World Champion and Australia's flagbearer at the Sochi Olympics in 2014.

Chumpy learned how to love from his parents, who simply adore and cherish each other. I'd never met a couple so together until I met them. The Pullins' sense of family was like nothing I'd ever known. And as close as Chump was with Chris and Sally, he was even closer to Emma. They wrote and played music together as Love Charli, and shared a secret sibling language of raised eyebrows and stifled smiles.

When we stepped inside, we immediately felt at home. Chumpy was brimming with excitement and started taking videos of every inch of the place. Meanwhile, I wanted to get out of there quick smart. The open house was packed with hopeful buyers. We didn't stand a chance.

'Come on, Chump, let's go. It's gonna hurt me to leave this house. I love it,' I eventually said, pushing him out the door before we could even ask the agent about the price guide because the house was clearly too nice for us.

As soon as we got into the car, Chumpy looked at me with a grin. 'We're going to get that house,' he said. 'I'll do whatever it takes, but we're getting that house.'

And we did. It took some number crunching, some serious bidding and a heartfelt letter to the real estate agent, but we got it. I couldn't quite believe it, but Chumpy never doubted it. He knew from the moment we got there that we'd found our place: our home. At the inspection, he mentally picked out which room he'd turn into his music studio, the corner of the yard he'd put a fire pit in and the spare room we'd turn into a nursery.

Chumpy filled the house with music, just like his parents had when he was a kid. We always had songs playing and our front door open, letting the breeze whip through. We both wanted our house to be a welcoming, warm space for all of our friends and family. It was a stunning spot and we wanted to share it with our loved ones – including my mum and brother, who moved to the area not long after us. Our home was their home.

Everyone knows the first step to making a house a home is getting a dog. I'd been campaigning long and hard for a dog when Chumpy surprised me with Rummi in 2018. I'd been down to Sydney for a friend's event, and came back to a new addition to the family – in the form of a kelpie. As much as I wanted a dog, I never would've chosen a kelpie! They're working dogs, they have too much energy and they can be anxious and stick-obsessed (so the arguments go). I wanted a fat, lazy dog I could cuddle. When I came home to puppy Rummi, I was annoyed for approximately one second. She was the sweetest puppy, all doe eyes and floppy ears, and we were obsessed with her.

Rummi was Chumpy's dog, man's best friend. They had such a special bond. Rummi would follow Chump around and he'd talk to her like a person. He put so much time and energy into training her, and she grew into the smartest dog in the world. We took her everywhere: on his parents' boat, to the café for coffee every morning and on holidays. But her favourite spot was in her dad's lap. Chumpy got into the habit of staying up for an extra twenty minutes after I went to bed so he could cuddle Rummi on the couch. It was sickeningly adorable how much they loved each other.

I know now that Chumpy chose Rummi for me. She's the most intuitive dog and she has so much of Chump in her: his caring nature, his obsession with the beach, his pure joy. Rummi knows the turn-off to her favourite beach in Tugun and as soon as I put the indicator on to turn in that direction, she starts to jump up and down and bark with excitement in the back of the car. Chumpy's light shines through in Rummi. She's still his dog.

Getting Rummi marked a whole new era for me and Chump. Our life was getting better and better every single day. Sometimes we'd just look at each other and say, 'How good is this?' We had the house, the dog and we were trying for the baby. There was so much to live for, so much good stuff to come, so many things to get excited about.

Chumpy's last Instagram post was a video of us and Rummi fanging around on his jetski the week before. His very first post, way back in 2013, was a blurry selfie of us in a car with the caption, *Two of us.*

I always knew how privileged I was in my life, and happy was my default setting. Nothing terribly awful had happened to me. I'd never lost someone close to me,

I hadn't battled a health scare, I wasn't consumed with worries. I woke up every morning excited for the day ahead – mostly because I woke up every morning next to Chumpy.

CHAPTER SIX

If Only

I always knew I'd be a mother.

It wasn't so much of a purpose or a calling, but a knowing. Having a baby was something I knew was in my future, in the same way I knew I would eventually get wrinkles and grey hairs: inevitable. I always knew I'd be a mother, and when I met Chumpy I knew he'd be the father of my kids.

It was something Chumpy and I talked about in the very early days. On our first holiday to Hawaii in 2013, we wrote a list of baby names.

Names ☼

Girls:	Boys:
Ava	*Bowie*
Evie	*Jerry*
Jagger Rose	*Banks*
Lyric	*Zeplin*
Maeve	

We'd been together six months. That might seem wildly quick to some people, but it felt right to us. We knew we were in love, that we were each other's person, that we wanted to be together forever.

We didn't need to be married to know that. Over the years, Chumpy and I had spoken about marriage and we both agreed it wasn't necessarily for us. We were already as together as you could be – we didn't need a piece of paper to prove it. Starting a family was much more important than walking down the aisle. While we loved going to our mates' weddings (Chumpy sang at everyone's weddings, including his friend and coach Ben's), we didn't feel the need to have one of our own. If anything, we would have eloped and had a ceremony, just the two of us, on a secluded beach somewhere.

When we were still living in Dee Why, my mum gave Chumpy my grandmother's wedding and engagement rings. She knew how committed he was to me and wanted to pass them down to us. It took us a few years, but we eventually decided to design a ring together with the jeweller Natalie Marie, who I knew. We created a stunning design using my grandma's diamonds and sapphires, but before we could get it made, Chumpy died.

Months later, a small box arrived in the post. It was from Natalie Marie. She'd made me the ring I'd designed with Chumpy. I wear it on my left hand, because even though I wasn't officially married to Chumpy, we'll always be together.

As much as I wanted to be a mum, I also wanted to see Chumpy as a dad. I knew within my bones that he'd be the greatest father – in the same way he was the greatest partner and the greatest dog owner; devoted, loving, fun and generous.

As usual, Chumpy wanted to be prepared – is anyone ever ready for a baby? – to have some savings and a house. He kept saying he'd do one more snowboarding season so in 2019, Chumpy was still competing, but after fifteen-odd years at the top, he started making plans for life after snowboarding.

We entered baby-making mode. It was game on. I was listening to a bunch of podcasts on fertility and pregnancy, and Chumpy was eating a heap of leafy greens and all the things they say are good for increasing sperm count. We were both being especially healthy, not that we'd ever been unhealthy – Chump always ate gluten-free and was conscious of what he put in his body – but we took it to the next level. I remember actually saying out loud to Chumpy, 'When I get pregnant, I'm not going to let myself go and eat crap. I'm going to be a crazy-healthy, annoying person and eat kale and drink green juices.'

Every month, we'd track my cycle and make the most of my fertility window. Every month, I'd get excited when I felt a twinge in my stomach … and every month I'd be gutted to realise the twinge was a period cramp. I found it quite cruel that periods mirrored the symptoms of pregnancy: sore boobs, bloating, even spotting could be a sign of cord implantation bleeding. It was such a headfuck.

One month, my period was late and we were so sure it was happening. This was the month it would stick. We went out and bought a set of tiny white Bonds baby singlets. They were so small and cute. It felt real.

I was sitting on the couch one night and Chumpy was beside me, rubbing my belly and talking to it.

'Who's in there?' he whispered. 'Are you a little boy or girl?' The idea was intoxicating. Two days later, I got my period.

After nine months of seriously trying to fall pregnant – and of me doing handstands after sex to improve our chances – Chumpy and I went to the doctor to get some tests done. We discovered his sperm was fine, but I had a low egg count. My heart sank. When the doctor showed us the graph and pointed to how low my egg count was compared to other people, it hurt. I couldn't help but feel guilty, even though I knew it was entirely out of my control. We were both devo and seeing Chump sad made me even sadder. I was worried, and frustrated with myself, but I tried to stay positive. Chumpy did the same. He was so supportive and encouraging.

The doctor tried to reassure me by reminding me that I was young and healthy. He said that even though I had a low egg count, my eggs were likely to be of good quality, and I clung onto that knowledge. I started doing acupuncture and Chumpy and I began talking about doing IVF. The doctor suggested we give it another few months and look at the IVF process after we'd been trying for a full year. I know a lot of couples try for a lot longer than we had been, so I wasn't overwhelmingly worried – we were still hopeful. We were actively trying to fall pregnant and considering all the options. A family was in our future and damn, we were excited about it.

I always knew I'd be a mother, but I never expected it to happen the way it did. I never expected I'd have to do it on my own.

Like the rest of the world, we didn't see 2020 coming. Chumpy and I started the year with such high hopes. In February we were together in Bali for the stunning wedding of our friends, Chloe and Fisher. It was a magical wedding full of love and laughs. Chump literally demonstrated why he is known as 'the wedding guy', because he is such a happy drunk and dances himself silly all night. He's always the king of the dance floor and he was at Chloe and Fisher's wedding too. At the end of the night, he and others jumped in the pool fully clothed.

After that we thought it was going to be *our* year. What fools!

When the pandemic struck and closed international borders and shut down snowboard competitions globally, we tried to make the most of it. For the first time in his adult life, Chumpy's schedule was empty, his passport was abandoned in his office drawer and his suitcase stayed unpacked. I'd been working for a high-end holiday rental company, and my work dried up as well. Chump and I joked about being 'funemployed' together, and we filled our days with all the things we loved: music, coffee, surfing with my brother, walking Rummi and entertaining at home. Chumpy also indulged in his new obsession: spearfishing. He'd normally head out with my brother or a mate, and return a few hours later with a feed for dinner.

One day, we caught an epic sunset and I gushed, 'Wow, look at that sunsetaroonie.' And so Chumpy's band name was born: Chumpy and the Sunsetaroonies. He thought the made-up word was a hoot, and it suited his reggae/rock/electro vibe. Chumpy called it a band, but really it was just him, writing every song, playing every instrument and producing every inch. I'd wake up most days to a freshly brewed coffee and music floating up the stairs from Chumpy's makeshift studio, where he'd spend hours tinkering on songs. I was sure music was going to be the next chapter in Chumpy's story. If he hadn't pursued snowboarding as a teenager, there's no doubt he would've been a musician.

On Sunday 5 July 2020, three days before Chumpy died, we spent the day at Fingal Beach with my friends Lizzo and Elly, Elly's partner, Westy, and our dogs. Chumpy and Westy jumped on their jetskis and headed over to Cook

Island just off the beach for a spot of spearfishing. Us girls went to get lunch and when we got back to the beach, we still hadn't seen or heard from the boys. It wasn't uncommon, but we started scaring each other as a joke. 'What if they don't come back?' we stirred. 'What if there's been a shark attack?' we gasped. 'What will we do?' we asked, jokingly. But we considered the answer and we agreed.

'Well, we'd rent out your house, Elly, and then you'd move in with me and Rummi, and we'd just become these weird widow dog mums together,' I said. When the boys came back late in the afternoon, we forgot all about our macabre plan.

Tuesday 7 July 2020 was regular in every way except one. Chloe and Fisher came over for dinner – fish tacos care of Chumpy's last spearfishing haul. Chloe is one of my best friends, and Fisher and Chumpy got on so well, but Fisher is an international DJ and was overseas as much as Chump. They were rarely in the country at the same time, so we made the most of any time together. We went to bed a little later than we normally would have on a Tuesday night. As usual, I went to bed first and Chump stayed on the couch cuddling Rummi for an extra twenty minutes before he slipped in next to me. It was a very nice, but super normal night in the Pullin household. We had no idea that those fish tacos would be Chumpy's last supper.

I carry so many what-ifs with me about that Wednesday morning. They are all-consuming. What if I told Chumpy he should go surfing instead of spearfishing? What if I bought him that diving watch he told me about, the one that could have tracked how long he'd been holding his breath? What if the sun had stayed behind the clouds on the morning of Wednesday 8 July instead of shining so damn bright? If only.

The last photo I took before my world stopped was of Rummi lying on Chumpy's side of the bed that morning, soaking up the body heat he'd left behind. Chumpy was downstairs, getting ready to go spearfishing, and I was still in bed with Rummi. In the shot, she looks alert with her ears up, almost as though she knew something bad was coming our way. I've spent so many hours staring at that photo, willing myself to go back to that time and place. I used to joke that the only good thing about Chumpy going away for work was that I got a break from being the weird third wheel, hanging out with him and Rummi. What I wouldn't give to be a third wheel again.

PART TWO

The After

'Find me at the bottom of the ocean,
find me at the bottom of the sea'

— Alex 'Chumpy' Pullin
'Sea Whiskers', lyrics by Love Charli, 2003

CHAPTER SEVEN

Numb

It was my brother who first mentioned it. The night of Chumpy's death, I was sitting in my backyard, on the edge of the deck with my head between my knees, when Dave sat down next to me and started talking. I only heard two words: 'sperm retrieval'.

My girlfriends Chloe and Laura had suggested it to him. At first, Chloe thought it was 'weird' and shut it down, but Laura pushed for her to speak to Dave. Laura had seen another friend of hers lose her partner when she was thirty. That friend was pregnant at the time, and she'd told Laura how much she wished she'd been able to retrieve her partner's sperm so she could give her son a sibling.

Those words ran through Laura's mind. 'This could save Ellidy's future,' she thought.

No-one knew if they should bring it up with me, let alone how. My brother probably agonised over how he'd tackle the subject, but he only had to say the words 'sperm retrieval' for me to know it was something I wanted to do. I'd never heard of post-mortem sperm retrieval and had no idea of the process or legalities, but I just knew. 'Yes,' I said to Dave without any hesitation. 'Do it. That's what I want. Can you make it happen? Please.'

Even though I didn't know what was involved, I had a feeling it was a time-sensitive situation. I wanted my brother to stop talking to me about it and do what needed to be done to make it happen.

I learned later that sperm can survive within the body for several days, but under current Queensland guidelines, sperm retrieval needs to happen within thirty-six hours. First we had to hire a fertility doctor from an IVF clinic to actually do the procedure and a lawyer to help with the legalities, so Bro and my friends hit the phones and started making calls.

Because Chumpy and I weren't married, his parents needed to sign an affidavit to give their support for the procedure. They were totally supportive of me and onboard with the idea. We were all in agreement that we'd do whatever we could to make the sperm retrieval happen then make any decisions later once the thick blanket of shock had lifted and we'd had time to think.

Time was ticking. The first handful of IVF clinics Chloe and Mum contacted didn't do sperm retrieval or weren't equipped to do it. I can't imagine what those conversations would have been like. 'Um, yeah, hi. My friend's boyfriend has just died. Can you retrieve his sperm for her?'

Finally, we got onto Doctor Andrew Davidson at a clinic in nearby Robina. He was very black and white about what had to happen. The process of getting the sperm was relatively simple – it involved making a cut and taking out sperm cells – but the red tape was less straightforward. We needed to speak to the coroner and get the green light before Doctor Davidson could do anything. I have no idea how many forms I signed during those precious hours.

It came down to the wire. We had thirty-six hours ... and the procedure happened in the thirty-seventh hour. Doctor Davidson went to the morgue and performed the retrieval at 9 pm. If he had been an hour later, or left it until business hours in the morning, it would have been too late. I felt like I was in the safest of hands – and so was Chumpy.

Somehow, against all odds, everything aligned that day for the sperm retrieval to happen. Had Chumpy died on a weekend, when courts and IVF clinics were closed, we wouldn't have been able to do it. I like to think Chumpy was helping us.

Once the sperm had been retrieved, it was taken back to Doctor Davidson's lab and examined. A scientist looked at it to see if there was any live sperm in the specimen. Only one per cent of the sperm was showing some sign of life, but that's all we needed: all it takes is a single sperm. The swimmers didn't need to be star athletes or perfect specimens, they just had to be alive. The only thing that mattered was that the sperm was viable and there was some hope in the shitshow that had become my life.

The sample was stored at the IVF clinic, and I put the thought of it on a shelf above my grief. It was always in the back of my head, but I didn't have the space to really think about it in those early days. I was in survival mode, doing what needed to be done in the moment, to just get through the day.

Later, Doctor Davidson's nurse, who happens to be his wife, told me she held Chumpy's hand and spoke to him during the procedure, telling him what they were doing and why.

'Oh shit,' I said, trying to imagine what that moment would have been like. 'So, like, he was just lying there, and you were holding his hand?'

'Yes, I talked him through the whole thing,' she said.

It was such a beautiful thing for her to do, and I felt so lucky to have her and her husband looking after me – and Chumpy. I knew it wasn't luck though, it was meant to be. Doctor Davidson was meant to do the procedure and be my IVF doctor. I felt like in their care, I was right where I was meant to be. It was also nice for me to know that Chumpy wasn't alone in that moment.

I was – and still am – eternally grateful to my brother, my mum and my friends for making the sperm retrieval happen, and to Chris and Sally for supporting it. It's not lost on me that the person responsible for Chumpy and me meeting at her twenty-first birthday party – Laura Enever – is also responsible for our baby.

It's also not lost on me how many women went before me to make sperm retrieval a reality. The first time a baby was born using post-mortem sperm was in 1999. Since then, the cases have been few and far between, but statistics from select sperm banks show they have increased in recent times.

There is no standard protocol for harvesting a dead man's sperm and in places where legislation exists, it varies widely. In Germany, Sweden, France, Canada and some states of Australia, the practice is banned entirely. Luckily, in Queensland, posthumous sperm donation is legal when a 'designated officer' is convinced the deceased wouldn't object and when the immediate family gives consent.

A 2014 US survey[*] found that seventy per cent of men aged eighteen to forty-four would want their spouse to be able to use their sperm after their death to have a baby, and that the presumption of consent would result in the dead men's wishes being honoured three times more often.

Some places require consent from the deceased partner to be given in writing, meaning a bloke would have to sit down and write, 'If I happen to die, I give permission for my missus to use my sperm to have our baby.' Unless someone was terminally ill or going off to fight in a war, I can't see that ever actually happening.

Chumpy's consent was clear in the last nine months of our lives – in the doctor's appointments we'd been to, in our research into IVF, in the conversations he'd had with his friends and family, in the home we bought and envisaged our babies growing up in, in the packet of tiny white Bonds baby singlets sitting unopened in our cupboard and in the list of baby names we wrote back in 2013 when we were on holiday in Hawaii.

---

[*] Posthumous gamete retrieval and reproduction: Would the deceased spouse consent? By Jason D. Hans, 2014, Social Science & Medicine Journal, https://www.sciencedirect.com/science/article/abs/pii/S0277953614005279

In 2017, a Queensland woman called Ayla Cresswell had to go to the Supreme Court to get permission to use the sperm of her late boyfriend, Joshua Davies, who had died very suddenly the year before. Ayla had the support of Joshua's family, evidence that he wanted to have children and affidavits from his friends saying the same. His sperm had been harvested within forty-eight hours of his death and stored at an IVF clinic, but Ayla needed the court's approval to use it. Almost a year after she launched her legal case, the judge granted her permission to use the sperm to attempt to have a baby. 'There is clear evidence that Joshua Davies expressed a desire to have children,' said Justice Brown in her ruling. 'I am satisfied that Ms Cresswell's decision is not an irrational response to grief ... [and] any child which may be conceived as a result of the use of Joshua Davies' sperm will be loved, cared for and able to be financially and emotionally supported, not only by Ms Cresswell but by the extended family.'

Ayla's case set a precedent. Because of her, I was able to do what I did.

Of course, not everyone agrees with posthumous reproduction. There are people who have moral, ethical or religious issues with using a dead person's sperm to have a child. People have been very vocal on Facebook about it, but I try not to read the comments. I like to think if people knew our story, knew how much Chumpy had wanted to have a child and knew how long we'd been trying, they would understand my decision. The idea of having a baby on my own and having a constant reminder of what I'd lost was hard enough without having to deal with other people's judgement. Until someone has been in my shoes, I don't think they'd ever be able to understand what I went through.

I know Chumpy would be cut up that his child doesn't have him in their life, but he would just love that a piece of him is still here, carrying on his name and his legacy. I know that because I know Chumpy.

In the midst of the turmoil of Chumpy's death in July 2020, I wrote a love letter to our baby, who didn't exist yet.

Dear baby Pullin,

I love you so much and you aren't even here yet.

Your dad is a warrior. He is absolutely beyond this world. He will be teaching you and guiding you. I may be the portal through which you learn from him. Maybe he will have direct access to you though.

You are wonderful and we are going on a journey. We need each other. Chump is taking us for a ride! An adventure. Truly magical.

This was a part of his soul contract. You and me, baby.
We live for him, through him and with him.

Love Mum xx

The shock stretched on and on. I was numb. I was a robot. I didn't cry constantly or collapse in a heap. I wondered if there was something wrong with me because I couldn't recognise that I was in complete and utter denial.

I think because Chumpy was away so much and I was used to being on my own, my brain tricked itself into thinking he was coming back. He wasn't *gone*, he just wasn't *here*. He could walk through the door at any second. These were the lies my mind told me. These were the lies I clung on to. These were the lies I knew weren't true.

They say there are five stages of grief – denial, anger, bargaining, depression and acceptance – and I was firmly stuck in the first phase. I felt like I was in a vortex where the world kept turning, but I stayed still. I was a fly on the wall, watching my grief, but not feeling it. I know if I saw what was happening to me in a film, I would've been a total, sobbing wreck watching it, but it was happening to me and I simply couldn't comprehend it.

I would walk down the street and see people out shopping and grabbing coffee, and think, 'How can everyone be going about their business like normal when Chumpy is gone?'

The feeling reminded me of a very specific moment from my youth. I remember standing in the middle of my local shopping centre, Warriewood Square, in 2008 when I found out Heath Ledger had died. I felt like screaming out to everyone, 'Don't you know that Heath Ledger is dead?' I didn't understand how life could go on when Heath Ledger was gone.

I felt the same bewilderment now but times one hundred. How could everything seem normal when Chumpy was gone?

If someone had asked me before how I would cope if Chumpy died, I would have said, 'Oh, I'd die too.' There's no way I could live without Chumpy. That was totally absurd. Impossible. But somehow, it was happening. Chumpy was dead, and I was still alive.

Reality hit me at the airport when I picked up Chumpy's parents the day after he died. I don't know how I drove from our house to Coolangatta airport. I definitely shouldn't have been on the road in my state. The same questions kept running through my mind, 'What's going on? What happened to Chump? What the actual fuck?' I made it to the airport in a daze.

Chumpy hated airports with a passion; they usually meant he'd be leaving me and Rummi to go to work. I wasn't thinking about that – or anything else – when I met Chris and Sal at the arrivals gate. They saw me – and I saw them – and we all fell in a heap. We held each other for a long time, not saying anything, just shaking. I had no idea how I was going to cope with my own feelings, let alone theirs. I couldn't give them any answers or comfort because I had none myself.

I didn't sleep much in the days after. At night, I started to obsessively take photos in our bedroom, looking for energy orbs and signs Chumpy was still with me. I felt him there, but I wanted to see him. I've never thought of myself as a 'spiritual' person and if you'd have told me a few months earlier that I'd be hunting for energy orbs, I would have rolled my eyes, but I found so much comfort in the thought of there being a spiritual dimension, the idea that there's something else beyond this physical plane, the fact that energy doesn't die, it just transforms. I felt Chump's energy the most in his music studio, in our bed and in Rummi. I took solace in the energy being calm and content. It was almost as though Chump was telling me, 'You'll be right, El.'

I'd walk Rummi at Tugun Beach at sunrise, not far from where Chumpy went for his last swim. It became my own form of therapy. I didn't talk, I just walked. And Rummi ran. She's a working dog and would only run when I gave her the command to 'go'. One morning, she took off running before I gave her the command. I looked at her racing to the far end of the beach and wondered, 'Who told you to go?'

Before Chumpy died, we watched the first season of Ricky Gervais's *After Life* together. In it, Ricky's recently bereaved character says he's only staying alive after the death of his wife because he has a dog to feed. It was strange to think we'd watched that show together, cuddling on the couch and laughing at the dark humour, and now, I was living it. I wasn't suicidal like Ricky's character, but if it wasn't for walking Rummi, I wouldn't have got out of bed every morning to face the day.

We all coped in our own way. While I was constantly on the lookout for signs from Chump, Em was building shrines to him in the bush on the outskirts of Wollongong, where she was living at the time. That's where she felt closest to her brother, out in nature. She was trying to create a place where she could visit him away from home. She created tributes to him out of tree branches, leaves and red candles and sent messages to Chumpy. He sent them back to her in the form of black cockatoos. Em kept seeing black cockatoos flying really low overhead, always in pairs. She liked to imagine they were her and him, flying high, but keeping low.

My friends and family rallied around me and held my head above the water when I wasn't strong enough to do it myself. I knew Chumpy was loved, but I'd had no idea how many lives he'd touched and how deeply his death would affect people the world over. I had messages from people far and wide, including from the waitress at our local café and a stranger who'd sat next to Chump on a flight and had never forgotten the way he lived his life with such fierce passion.

Three days after Chumpy died, our friend Chris Enever, Laura's brother, organised a paddle out at Narrabeen Beach in Sydney. More than 500 people turned out in the middle of winter to honour Chumpy. One of Chump's best mates and fellow snowboarder Nate Johnstone spoke at the back of the surf in a circle of mourners. 'Chump, you were taken from us far too early. However, your time here was not wasted and your approach to life was infectious. The legacy you've left behind is something to be admired and it's an inspiration to so many. But who you were to me was the person I looked up to most and I'm so proud to call you my friend,' he said, through sobs. 'I know you're up there looking down on us with a smile and the support you have here today shows how much you were loved.

The world needs more people like you in it. Our time for making new memories has passed, but the ones we have, we will hold forever in our hearts. I love you like a brother, rest easy, you will never be forgotten. To Chump!'

The crowd splashed and cheered and threw flowers into the ocean for Chump.

That same weekend, we had our own paddle out at Palm Beach in Queensland. There's a photo of me on my knees in the sand looking totally and brutally distraught; I have no memory of that moment. I do remember paddling out alongside my closest friends (some of whom had travelled up from Sydney), my brother and Chumpy's parents. In the water above the reef where my soulmate spent his final moments, we formed a circle, sitting on our surfboards. Bro paddled into the middle and said some words. I sat shaking and crying, my face salty with seawater and tears.

Bro and I were the last ones to come back to shore. We stayed out there until my body was as numb as my mind. On the way back into the beach, I caught a nice little wave and it felt like Chumpy had sent it to me. 'Here you go, Elmo,' I imagined him saying. 'This one's for you.'

Chumpy's obituary was a testament to the man he was. It read:

A life full of love, well lived.

On 8 July, 2020, at the age of 32, Alex 'Chumpy' Pullin, loving partner, son and brother, passed away peacefully at 'Chumpy's Reef' on 19th Ave, Palm Beach.

Chumpy was born on 20 September, 1987 in Benalla, Victoria to Chris and Sally Pullin. Adventure was ingrained in his blood from a young age, going on his first family sailing trip to Lord Howe Island at three months old. At the age of three, he was on skis, by eight he was riding a snowboard, and in the year Chumpy turned 15, he was crowned national boardercross champion. This set him on a lifelong path of travel, adventure and competition that peaked with winning World Championships in 2011 and 2013. Chumpy represented Australia at three Olympic Games, and in 2014 was the nation's flagbearer in Sochi, Russia. In a sport-mad country like Australia, honours don't come much higher.

But Chumpy was more than an athlete, so much more.

It was the birth of his sister Emma when Chumpy was three years old that would spark his second major passion, music. Music was a family affair in the Pullin household and Chumpy took huge inspiration from the entire family, especially his mum, Sally, and Em, going on to form

119

multiple bands with the latter, the music that we're all witnessing today.

His third and arguably most precious passion point, his beloved El. A love that truly knew no bounds, a love that we all dream of. El and Chump met, where so many of our most cherished memories are, on the dance floor. This kicked off an almost decade-long life of love, adventure, a beautiful pup in our perfect little Rummi and a happiness that made so many of us envious.

Chumpy was a genuine human with an energy and passion for life that could only be described as infectious and inspiring.

A man with boundless amounts of talent combined with a fearless and unapologetic determination to succeed, Chumpy became a hero to so many people around the world.

Alex was known as a snowboarder, Olympian, surfer, ocean lover, musician, media personality and dancer, but it is the strength of his character, the way he carried himself and led his life that we will remember most.

A person who lit up every room that he entered, lent an ear when you needed it the most, was there to pick you up with his endless positivity and love no matter if you were lifelong friends or had just met.

A legacy is etched into the minds and hearts of others, and the stories they share about you. We promise to continue your legacy, never forgetting what you stood for, living each day with a big smile and even bigger heart.

He will be greatly missed by his loving family, friends and his beautiful El. Forever in their hearts.

The outpouring of love was overwhelming. Looking back, I like to think that other people carried my pain for me. Being numb didn't make me a sociopath; I was being shielded from a loss so huge it would have swallowed me whole if I'd felt the full force all at once. In the rare moments I found myself alone, I collapsed. I fell to my knees and let it all out. My loved ones held me together.

Mum and Lizzo moved in with me, and there was a constant stream of people coming through the front door, checking in, dropping off home-cooked meals and asking what they could do to help. I remember being happy to see old friends, only to notice the tears in their eyes and realise why they were visiting me: Chumpy was dead. I couldn't say the word 'dead' for a very long time, more than a year. It still doesn't feel right coming out of my mouth. The word still sticks to my tongue, and I have to force it out.

Emma arrived on the Gold Coast a couple of days after her parents. It was the first time she'd been to our house. Chumpy was always video-calling her and showing her around, so she knew what everything looked like, but she hadn't had a chance to visit us, something she regrets to this day. I could tell how hard it was for her being in Chumpy's home without Chumpy there. I felt the same – lost. When Emma walked inside, her mum was playing Chumpy's ukulele in his music studio. If ever there was a sight to break your heart …

I was standing outside the funeral home when I decided I didn't want to see Chumpy's body. People had tried to convince me to see him, telling me he just looked like he was sleeping and that it might give me some closure, but I knew I couldn't handle seeing him and knowing he wasn't *there*. He was gone.

Chris and Sally took Rummi to see Chumpy. Apparently, she jumped up to look in the coffin, had a quick glance and immediately ran outside. If Chump had still been there, she never would have left his side. He was gone. His soul being was not inside his body anymore. The funeral home had washed him with some kind of disinfectant and he smelled sterile. I wondered if Rummi could still smell her dad or if he was a stranger to her in that moment.

I think it's natural for humans to seek out some sort of explanation for the unimaginable, to find meaning in loss, to justify tragedies as being part of a bigger plan. What happened to Chumpy couldn't just be an accident – it had to mean something. I found a quote that rang true for me:

'A flame that burns twice as bright, burns half as long.' But philosophical musings don't keep you warm at night. They don't kiss you on the forehead and they sure as hell don't make you a cup of coffee in the morning.

I still had so many questions, not just about what happened and why it happened, but about how on earth I was going to survive without Chump. How was I meant to find light when my bright flame had been put out? How could I keep breathing when it felt like all of the air had been sucked out of the world? How could my heart possibly be expected to keep beating when there was such a massive hole in it?

I don't think I'll ever understand why it happened. Why was Chumpy taken? Why not me? I'll never make sense of it. I'll never not be sad, and I'll never not be grieving his loss.

CHAPTER EIGHT

A Loving Partner, Son and Brother

I wore white to Chumpy's funeral. We had it outside, at the Melaleuca Station Memorial Gardens in Chinderah. Maybe because of the beautiful surroundings, I kept calling it 'the wedding' instead of 'the funeral'.

'I need to write a speech for the *wedding*,' I'd say. 'Do you think we can ask Red Bull to help stream the *wedding* for anyone who can't get here?' I'd say the same things over and over again. 'God, I hope everyone can make it to the *wedding*. We should organise a video stream of the *wedding*, just in case.'

At twenty-eight, I should have been marrying the love of my life – not burying him. I didn't want to be planning a fucking funeral, but I was. I didn't want to be a widow, but I was.

I had a lot of help with all the arrangements. I think everyone wanted to be productive, to feel like they were doing something to be a part of it. It wasn't something Chumpy and I had ever spoken about. When you're young, fit and healthy, you don't tend to talk about your final wishes or what you want for your funeral. I tried my best to think about what mattered most to Chump. I knew he'd want the funeral to be outside in the sunshine, that he'd want his music to be playing and that he'd want to be cremated.

Laura and her brother Chris, who was the MC at the funeral, caught an Uber to the venue. When they got in the car, the driver told them he had been planning to knock off early, but their job came through at 11.11 am, so he'd picked it up. The driver explained he was actually a psychic medium doing Uber on the side.

'Where are you guys off to today?' the driver asked.

'We're actually going to our friend's funeral,' Chris said, struggling to believe the words.

'Oh, okay. Well, there's a guy in the car with us and he's saying it's okay and good luck,' the driver replied. 'Why would your mate be saying good luck?'

Laura and Chris were taken aback.

'I'm actually the MC for the day and I'm pretty nervous,' Chris explained.

'Well, he's saying you're going to be fine, that you're ready for it,' the driver continued. 'He's also saying that it happened underwater, but he wants you to know he's okay.'

Chris and Laura just looked at each other in amazement and a fair bit of shock. The Uber driver was right on both accounts – Chris was fine and he did a beautiful job. The next day, the driver got Chris's number from the booking and called him.

'Hey, I didn't tell you this yesterday, but when you jumped out of the car at Melaleuca Gardens, I was sitting in the car, waiting for another ride, when a white car pulled up beside me and a woman got out wearing a white outfit and a white hat,' he said, perfectly describing me. 'Your friend [who had passed] was still in the car with me and he told me, "That's my girl and that's my dog. I will be coming through in my dog today."'

He wasn't wrong: Rummi wore bright flowers around her collar at the funeral and lovingly did the rounds, checking on everyone during the service. It was like she knew who needed to pat her in each moment. So many people told me they thought Chumpy was in Rummi's body that day – just like the Uber driver said.

Baden Donegal, the lead singer of Ocean Alley, opened the funeral with an acoustic performance of their song 'Knees'. Chumpy loved Ocean Alley and he loved that song. Baden sat in the sun with his guitar on his lap and sang a song about being brought to his knees. It took all of my strength not to collapse onto the ground.

I wrote my eulogy for Chumpy in our bed, in the early hours of the morning in the days before, when I couldn't sleep for fear of waking up to another day without him. I wrote it like a twenty-first speech instead of a funeral tribute. I wrote it to make Chumpy laugh.

I'm a terrible public speaker, and I should have been nervous standing in front of such a big crowd, but I wasn't. It felt like I was just talking to myself in the mirror. When I went up to speak, I was too tall for the microphone so I slipped my heels off and felt the grass under my feet. I was grounded, but I felt like I was floating outside my body, watching from above. Bro stood beside me with his arm around my shoulder, as though he knew, as though he was trying to stop me floating away, to be with Chump.

The words spilled out of my mouth, punctuated by tears and laughs.

Chump, the lyrics you and Em wrote when you were 16 couldn't be more real:

'Find me at the bottom of the ocean, find me at the bottom of the sea.

Find me in the orchard of desire, that's where I'll always be.'

Chump, you'd always question and evaluate life every day. You thought critically, loved deeply and created passionately, forever evolving and learning, trying to do better and to be better for us. You are everything and more. You are perfect. I wish I could grab you and tell you that one more time.

I always called you my Viking or my ninja because you are so strong and capable. There literally isn't one thing you can't do, except golf. And going to the supermarket alone. You used to call it 'the superfuckit'.

The birthday card you made me in May this year says, '2020 is our year. How fucking good is our life Elmo? I'm not sure how it can get better from here, but I know it will.'

I will hold onto these words forever. I promise to somehow make you proud.

My heart aches knowing I won't be able to wake up to your beautiful music beaming up the stairs from your studio or the morning coffee or seeing the stoke on your face grow bigger as each morning you'd improve.

I'm going to miss your random improv breakouts and the nights where Bro and I would bully you into prank calling Dad with your outstanding Kiwi accent and trying to sell him adult nappies over the phone.

The past six months has been nonstop adventure. With Covid, you've not been travelling and I've been out of work. We surfed with Bro pretty much every day before it got too cold, and you guys would call me a pussy. While everyone else was hating 2020, we were absolutely frothing. How good was being 'funemployed' together?

One of my favourite standout memories this year was when we were surfing Currumbin Alley with Bro. I'd sit out on the shoulder while Bro and Chumpy would get all the bombs. Bro caught a wave and was heading straight for me. I was like, 'Yew, Bro!'

And he was yelling at me as he always is, 'Paddle, paddle, paddle, get this one with me, don't be a pussy.'

I didn't. And of course I felt like a kook. Then Chump caught the next wave, by my standards it was huge, but the tide was pretty full and giving me the confidence, plus I already felt like a kook for missing

Bro's wave. So I paddled. I yelled, 'Chumpo, I'm coming too.'

As I dropped in on him, he was so stoked. I could see how proud he was. He was like, 'Yes El, fuck yeah.' We rode this little – I thought it was massive – right-hander all the way to shore together and we even held hands together at the end like little grommets. It was the best. Pure happiness. We couldn't wait for Bro to come in so we could share our stoke with him.

Chump imitated me the whole rest of that afternoon, 'Chumpo, I'm coming too, Chumpo.' That day was also when Chumpy decided his new nickname of Chumpo – that me and a bunch of the girls had decided to call him the past few months – wasn't so bad. Better than Chumperelli.

The man was annoyingly perfect. You could see it pissed people off. He'd constantly remain humble and unassuming so that the rest of us would feel less like clowns.

Chump would learn a song overnight and it would sound identical to the original, that we'd be like, 'Hmm, it's a bit boring, you sound exactly like Neil Young, it's a bit too good.' So I made him learn 'Window Shopper' by 50 Cent because surely he wasn't about to turn gangster. When I think back, though, I reckon he gave it a crack when I wasn't home.

If there was something he hadn't accomplished, you bet he'd YouTube it, learn it, practise it, perfect it straightaway. He would suddenly become a web developer or an electrician overnight. He fused together our broken TV cables with sparks. I'd never have any words other than, 'That'd be fucking right.'

I would do anything right now for one of your long-arse life chats where we're lying in bed and I'm about to fall asleep. No matter how tired I am, I promise this time I won't say, 'Can you just email me the rest of this story?'

Everyone knows how I feel about him, but I don't actually think words do it justice. He was the most positive, energetic and happy person. Us having fun and being happy was his priority above all. He was a complete go-getter, my rock. He was also my encyclopedia and dictionary because he just knows everything there is to know without being a dickhead about it. If I don't know something, surely Chumpo would.

I promise you Chumpy, I will put one foot in front of the other. I will keep going for our family, for

Rummi, for our home sanctuary that we created. Our house will not fall apart. I'll get that whipper-snipper out. You'll be watching down on me completely butchering it and expect nothing less, I'm sure.

Stay with us Chump. Keep moving oceans. Keep showering us with your beauty through butterflies, rainbows, birds and more. I want to feel you around me forever. I'd do anything right now for one of those inconvenient, long-arse, ten-minute cuddles when I'm right in the middle of something and you squeeze me so hard to stop me squirming. I would cling on forever, baby.

Thank you for showing me what true, unconditional love is. I feel so blessed and lucky to have shared this rare, magical connection with you.

Rumbledore and I promise to make you proud and never stop learning.

We love you forever.

The wake was held at the Currumbin Beach Vikings Surf Club, looking out at the same stretch of ocean where Chumpy died. We could only have 120 people in the venue, so the overflow threw down blankets on the sand and cracked a beer to watch the sunset. Chumpy put on a good one for us.

I heard new stories about Chump and ones I'd heard a dozen times before. There was the one about a six-hour road trip of nonstop singing through Austria with Nam Baldwin, his performance coach. The night Chump shared a tiny hotel room on tour with Cam and how they went to bed at 7.30 pm to be ready for an early start the next day, only to spend five hours deep in conversation. And, of course, all the not-so-secret man crushes so many blokes had on him.

Everyone was distraught, but my dad seemed especially lost. He and Chumpy were similar in so many ways. They both had a childlike spirit, were larger than life and possessed a flair for theatrics. Chumpy loved to tell a story about running into my dad at the local RTA in Warriewood Square shopping centre not long after they'd met for the first time.

'I was waiting in line at the transport office and this guy came up to me and tapped me on the back,' Chumpy would say. 'Then he pulled out a possum from his shorts' pocket in the middle of the shopping centre and said, "Shh, I'm not allowed to have this in here," as he put the possum back in his pocket, like it was the most normal thing to be carrying around.' Chumpy was fascinated by Dad, and Dad revelled in having an audience.

Dad had survived two minor heart attacks, both of which occurred after having a few beers and eating a Vindaloo curry (you'd think he might have learned his lesson after the first Vindaloo floored him!). He was a force of nature, so to see him like a shell of a person was hard.

At the funeral, people noticed Dad was off. I noticed it too, earlier in the week when Dad arrived and we went to see Bro at his house around the corner. I insisted on driving because I didn't feel comfortable with Dad behind the wheel. He was vague, a bit wobbly on his feet and totally not himself. We all chalked it up to grief. Hell, I was vague, wobbly and out of sorts too.

I don't really remember seeing or speaking to anyone in particular that day. Like so much of that time, the day was a blur. I know I would have talked and hugged and cried on the shoulders of so many people, but all the shoulders have blended into one in my memory. All I know is that not one of those shoulders was Chumpy's.

In the days and weeks after the funeral, reality slowly started to creep in: I was a widow. The grief snuck up on me. It hit at the most mundane moments. The first time I had to mow the lawn and clean up the yard, I broke down. Chumpy loved to whipper-snip and – as he was with everything – he was a perfectionist about it. I cursed at the mower and the whipper-snipper that I had to cut the grass on my own, that Chumpy wasn't there to do it and I quickly went back on my word and decided *fuck that, I'm getting someone in to do this job.* Chump would have hated seeing me mess up the lawn. And I hated doing it. I knew he'd be upset that I was missing spots.

Every morning, the coffee machine was an unassuming reminder that Chumpy would never make me a coffee again. The bamboo Chumpy planted outside our kitchen window to block out the view of the neighbour's fence was a reminder that Chumpy never got to see it grow. The pool that Chumpy took such pride in cleaning was a reminder that life went on – the leaves kept falling and the chores still needed doing, even now that Chumpy wasn't there to do them.

I was alone in the house Chumpy loved, surrounded by vases of flowers. After Chumpy died, the flower deliveries came thick and fast. My pantry is still full of vases that my friends had to run out to Kmart to buy because we didn't have enough for all the flowers. I used to love receiving flowers; now the sight of them hurts my heart.

Before and after the funeral, I was sent messages, unexpected gifts and words of support. Snowboarding coach, Peter Baff, arranged for an incredible artist named Ed, who goes by the name 'Breathe A Blue Ocean', to draw a mural of Chumpy and Rummi in the sand on the beach at Ocean Grove and for photographer Adam Stan to capture the masterpiece from a drone above. The framed print hangs at the top of my stairs.

For the first World Cup without Chumpy, his fellow snowboarders held a moment of silence for him. One of his greatest rivals, Pierre Vaultier from France, created a digital portrait of Chumpy using strategically placed colour-coded photos of his snowboarding family to honour his legacy and all that he did for the sport.

Australian poet Leanne Laydon, who goes by sunburntpoet, wrote a number of poems dedicated to me and Chumpy. Including this one.

One More Day
I can count the hours since I saw you
And I just want one more day
One more kiss, one more 'I love you'
One more day without this pain
One more picnic on the headland
One more swim at our favourite beach
One more night under the moonlight
Tangled in our sheets
This wasn't meant to happen
And there's no words to explain

How our lifetime of tomorrows
Became memories from yesterday
I just want one more day
I would give anything, my love
If I can't have you tomorrow
Then just today would be enough

I didn't know how to grieve. I had never experienced a loss like this, so I didn't know where to start. I stopped short of googling 'How to grieve,' but I did all the things I thought I should do: I made an appointment with a counsellor, I cuddled my dog, I went through the motions – but I still couldn't feel the emotions. There was nothing going on behind my eyes. I was vacant.

My first grief counsellor must have thought I'd lost the plot. 'Why are you here today?'

'Well, my boyfriend just died. He was spearfishing when he had a shallow water blackout. We were able to retrieve his sperm, though, so I'm going to have his baby,' I said on autopilot. I was totally matter-of-fact, like I was describing the plot of a very sad film.

I think I thought that if I went to enough counselling sessions and a grief retreat and ticked all the boxes that it'd be okay and I wouldn't be sad. It might even all go away. That's not how grief works, though. You can't squeeze it into a nice little box and wrap a bow around it. You can only ride it out. And it's a shit ride.

Just a few weeks later, I spent a weekend at a grief retreat at Uki in far northern New South Wales. It was too much too soon. I wasn't ready for it. I feel like I would get a lot more out of the experience if I were to do it again now. The word 'journey' feels like such a cliché, but that's what grief is. It's an ongoing process, and there isn't a destination. You can't win at grief.

The best part of the retreat for me was that it was tech-free, so I spent three days without my phone. I couldn't endlessly scroll through photos of Chumpy and I wasn't being sent daily reminders of what we were doing on this day five years earlier.

For the most part, though, I felt entirely out of place. Because I was still in denial and numb to my emotions, I felt like I didn't deserve to be sitting in the circle alongside all the other people who'd lost loved ones.

My brain was working overtime to protect me. I couldn't cope with the reality, so I disconnected from it altogether.

CHAPTER NINE

His Father's Hero – by Chris Pullin

In Viking history, Ragnar Lothbrok was a farmer who became a fierce warrior who led the invasion of the British Isles and Holy Roman Empire and was crowned King of Denmark and Sweden. His wife, Lagertha, was a shield-maiden who became the ruler of Norway. It was a brutal time.

Chumpy was always fascinated by the stories of the Vikings, and they influenced the way he competed. Before a race, I'd tell him to channel his inner Ragnar. 'Go out and rip someone's fucking head off,' I'd say, and he would. On the track, of course.

The boat we had in 2020 was called *Lagertha*. She was a beautiful 55-foot cruiser with classic timber finishes and a sunbaking deck. Chumpy and Ellidy spent many happy days on the old girl, catching crayfish and watching dolphins swim in her wake.

The last time I saw my son was when he dropped us off at the marina. We said goodbye at the dock. Sally and I had just spent three days with Chumpy and Ellidy at their place, and we were sailing north from Tweed Heads to deliver *Lagertha* to her new owners. We'd had a wonderful stay with our boy. El was aways such a generous host – they both made a real fuss of us – and the energy in the home was warm and joyous. It made saying goodbye all the more difficult. It was a heartfelt farewell, and I'll admit I got a bit teary watching as Chumpy walked down the dock, back to his car. I can still picture the moment.

I don't know what possessed him, but after we'd said our goodbyes and he'd started to head off, Chumpy stopped, turned around and came back for another hug. I've replayed that hug in my head over and over, like a well-loved record. It was the last time I saw my son alive.

We were back at our home in Eden when we heard ...

'It's El,' she said. She sounded distant, like she wasn't really there. What she said next made my knees weak. 'I think Chump's had an accident.' She stumbled over her words. 'I'm not sure, but I think he's died. I don't know.'

'Oh no. No, that can't be right. It's impossible,' I replied. I'd heard what Ellidy had said, but I couldn't understand it. It couldn't be true; it just couldn't. My son couldn't be dead.

I went into shock. I don't remember hanging up the phone or relaying the message to Sally. I know we drove to Sydney airport the next day, but I have no recollection of the seven-hour trip. I know some friends met us at the airport to take care of our car so we could get straight on a plane to the Gold Coast, but I don't know what we said to them.

News had broken overnight that Olympic snowboarder Alex 'Chumpy' Pullin had died in a spearfishing accident at Palm Beach. When we boarded the flight, the flight attendant looked a bit gloomy when she checked our boarding passes and she seated us in the business class section despite us only having economy tickets.

When we walked into Chumpy and Ellidy's house, our son wasn't there. The place was full of people, but it felt empty. The dining room where we'd shared a happy meal less than a fortnight earlier was eerily cold. We didn't feel like we were in our son's home – the home we watched him proudly buy, that we'd dropped off our teak outdoor table setting to, that we'd helped organise the solar panels for. We felt numb and distant from it all.

Conversations were happening all around us, but we weren't involved. It was like we were witnessing – but not participating in – the moment. I kept waiting for Chumpy to walk through the front door and ask what everyone was doing in his lounge room. I stared at the door, willing it to happen, praying, wishing.

My heart was broken into a million pieces, and seeing Ellidy's utter devastation shattered it into a million more. She went from being the happiest girl in the world to the saddest. It was the most extraordinary loss. We loved Ellidy for the simple reason that we loved Chumpy and he chose her, but once we got to know her, we loved her all on our own. Seeing her pain amplified our own pain.

The same went for Emma. When we first called Em to tell her something had happened to Chumpy, she was at work at the creative studio where she does screen printing. Her boss took one look at her after she got off the phone and knew something was wrong. When she told him what I'd said, they both agreed it couldn't be Chumpy. It just couldn't.

'It's him,' I said when I called Em back. She had to steady herself on the windowsill outside the studio because she went into shock.

Em was based in Wollongong at the time and it took her longer than us to get to the Gold Coast, so we were relaying what was happening to her in between sobs on phone calls. Em's grief was all-consuming. She stopped breathing on 8 July 2020, and I don't know if she'll ever start again. She didn't just lose a brother, she lost her best friend and a part of herself.

None of it felt real, not even when Sally and I went to see Chumpy's body in the funeral home, not even when we discussed cremation, not even today. I don't know if the reality will ever sink in.

In the sterile viewing room, Sally put her hand on Chumpy's chest. I held on to her. At any second, I thought we might both drop to the ground under the weight of our heartache. We talked to Chumpy for about fifteen minutes. We didn't want to leave, to say goodbye; we didn't want it to be the last time we saw our son. I pictured Chumpy turning around on the dock and coming back to hug us one last time and I wished with everything I had to go back to that moment, to feel my son's arms around me again, to tell him I loved him once more.

Seeing Chumpy that one last time is not something I regret, but it's also not something I'd recommend. I don't think people should or shouldn't view the body of their loved one after a tragedy. It's such a personal decision. There isn't a right or wrong choice. Ellidy chose to not see Chumpy and that was right for her. We couldn't miss out on the opportunity to see him, even if he was cold to touch.

When I close my eyes and picture my son, I don't picture his lifeless body in the funeral home – I can, but I don't. Instead, I see him grabbing me by the shoulders and telling me that he loves me.

I was a rip-and-tear father. When the kids were teenagers and we were driving together down the road on our property between the house and the shed, I used to slam on the handbrake to put the ute in a spin and make the kids scream. It always got a good reaction and I loved seeing the looks on their faces.

When he was old enough to drive, Chumpy came home one afternoon and sheepishly confessed he'd damaged a tyre and rim on the ute. You can guess how he did it! He'd come down the dirt lane that led to our house and chucked a handbrakey but, unfortunately, he mistimed it and hit the back wheel on the culvert on the edge of the road. Both Chump and Em looked very unhappy with themselves and apprehensive about my response. What could I say? I was the one who taught him how to do a handbrakey. 'Mate, you better line it up right next time,' I said and left it at that.

That's what a dad should do: teach his son how to spin the wheels on the ute without roughing up the back rim. A father shouldn't have to write his son's eulogy. It's entirely unnatural. It goes against human nature. The young bury the old; that's how it goes.

And yet, somehow, I found myself writing Chumpy's eulogy and reading it out at his funeral.

The first time I met Chumpy, a nurse placed him, wet and slimy, on Sally's sweaty tummy. His head was up. Wriggling and crawling, he climbed up. His tiny hand reached out and closed around Sally's nipple. Love exploded in our hearts. I couldn't feel the ground.

Our home was full of music. Sally's guitar became Chumpy's. Every day, Emma and Chumpy playing and writing songs. We all hated school, we made music and we went on crazy adventures, the four of us. We didn't care about the world; we were our world.

Sally and I absolutely loved those years with Chumpy and Emma, man, we had some times. At fourteen, he did his first solo mission to the US. The

*plan was to try and break into the international
world of snowboard cross. A snowboard in a bag,
no phone, hopefully enough money. The first of so
many trips, eventually to pretty much every place in
the world that had snow. Being a part of his racing
was a rush. Always training, evolving and winning.
We rode his wave of success, the highs and the lows,
and always we had the beautiful music. Always, the
songs.*

*We loved the energy which flowed from him. It
was infectious and he would bring us along just for
the ride. Then one wonderful night, he met Ellidy. He
knew it, right from the beginning, crazy love. Once
on* Sea Whiskers, *he told me, 'Dad, Elli is the one.'*

*Elli and Chump became the dream team. He was
so very happy, so much in love. With Elli, he was
a better man. She calmed him, softened, made him
more compassionate. Chumpy could see their future
and he liked it a lot. Wonderful Rummi, lovely Elli
and the happiest guy in the world.*

*I absolutely know that Chumpy's life
achievements, while spectacular, were only the
beginning. He was only just getting warmed up,
planning a family. We were about to see Chumpy's
bright light turn to sun and illuminate us all in his*

warm glow as a dad. My tears are not for me, but for
El and Chumpy. I am so unbearably sorry.
Chumpy always made me walk taller. Feller boy,
I'll see you out there.

Chumpy had a tattoo on his arm of a skeleton figure smoking a pipe and carrying a bindle, framed by the words, 'See you out there'. On one of his last visits to our home in Eden, Chumpy sat down with me and we drew up a sketch for our dream boat. After he died, we finished building the boat – and named her *See you out there*. It's simultaneously a beautiful reminder of our time on the water together and a sucker punch that Chumpy is no longer with us. He'll never see the boat or jump off the side into the sea with his sister or take his kids on family trips. That thought isn't just tragic; it's fucking agony.

The pain of our son's funeral was made worse by the fact many of our family and friends from Victoria couldn't be there with us because of lockdowns. The people at the funeral loved him dearly, but they didn't know him as a baby, as a young boy, as a nephew, grandson or grommet. It felt unfair that we had to face the funeral without our family, that they couldn't grieve beside us.

The snowboarding community was also in mourning. We had messages, emails and letters from all over the world. At home, Geoff Lipshut made a heartfelt tribute by naming the recently renovated athlete accommodation at the Olympic Training Centre at Mount Buller 'Chumpy's Lodge'. The lodge was somewhere Chumpy had spent plenty of time over the years, and now his memory will live on there. In his dedication speech, Geoff said Chumpy was the best he'd ever met, the most professional athlete and the nicest person. 'Chumpy genuinely believed that anything was possible, which is why he was so important to the athletes of his generation, and through Chumpy's Lodge, generations to come,' Geoff said.

On what would have been Chumpy's thirty-third birthday in September 2020, we lit a bonfire in his honour at our place in Eden and invited everyone who couldn't make it to the funeral. The flames licked the crisp night air and the smoke rose to the stars. I wrote Chumpy a letter and read it out in the glow of the fire. Then I threw it into the flames and watched it burn.

In Viking times, pyre funerals were common. A wooden structure was built to hold the corpse and grave offerings, and to make the pillar of smoke as tall as possible in order to lift the deceased to the afterlife. The custom is explained in the 'Ynglinga Saga' by Icelandic poet and historian Snorri Sturluson:

Thus he [the almighty Odin] established by law that all dead men should be burned, and their belongings laid with them upon the pile, and the ashes be cast into the sea or buried in the earth. Thus, said he, everyone will come to Valhalla with the riches he had with him upon the pile.

The bonfire burnt until the early hours of the morning, until the flames turned to embers and the night sky turned to dawn.

CHAPTER TEN

Screaming Under Water

The day before Chumpy passed, we'd gone out and left Rummi at home. When we got back, our neighbours came over and told us she'd been howling. We didn't believe it at first – Rummi only barks in excitement, she'd never howled in her life – but our neighbours swore it was her. They'd even looked over our fence to check, because it was so out of character for her, and seen Rummi sitting on the deck, howling to the sky.

We didn't think much of it at the time, but the memory came flooding back to me two months later when I was visiting my dad in Sydney and Rummi started howling again. I started filming and imitating her because it was so unusual and, I thought, funny. I was laughing, but my dad was stone-faced.

'Can you stop her howling? I don't like it,' he said, more earnest than I'd ever heard him.

'Why?' I asked.

'I just don't think it's a good sign when dogs howl,' he explained. 'It means something bad is going to happen.'

I thought about dogs howling at fireworks and sirens and thunder and realised Dad had a point. I decided to look it up, and the first result on Google said, 'dogs howl when death is near'. I got goosebumps.

A month after Chumpy died – and after Rummi howled for the first time – my dad was diagnosed with glioblastoma of the brain, which is an extremely aggressive form of cancer. Rummi was howling again, and I wondered if she could smell the cancer in Dad and knew that he was dying.

Dad's cancer was stage four – the end. There was no going back. There was no miracle cure. One of the most brutal things about glioblastoma is that the symptoms don't generally present until it's too late. Dad was experiencing dizziness, fatigue and confusion. A scan found a massive tumour on his brain. The doctors said he might not make it to Christmas.

I couldn't believe it. Dad and Chumpy both had such an enormous presence; I couldn't imagine a world without both of them. Surely the hole they'd leave would swallow me up. I wondered why I'd gone my whole life without losing anyone close to me, and why death was now following me. I wondered if I was cursed and if the men in my life should steer clear of me. I wondered.

When they were together, my dad and Chumpy bounced off each other. Their energy filled the room. My dad brought back a fake wooden penis bottle opener thingo from a market stall in Bali and they'd use it as a microphone when they did karaoke together, thinking they were hilarious. Chumpy was naturally talented at performing, and my dad was ... confident. He didn't have the best voice but he had rhythm and was fully committed to every song and dance move. Dad was a showman. After he left the police force, he essentially retired and became Holiday Pete. He took up modelling and did advertisements for Toyota, but he spent most of his time riding his motorbike up and down the coast, travelling all over and living life to the fullest. Dad was a ball of energy, and I didn't want to live in a world without that energy.

I had such a special connection with my dad. He used to call me the Elli-copter, because I'd spin into his house in a whirlwind. After we moved to the Gold Coast, I'd fly down and surprise Dad whenever I could. I'd get a friend to pick me up from the airport and drop me off at his place so I could sneak up on him. I'd pop up out of nowhere and scare the hell out of him. He loved it.

In August 2020, shortly after Dad got his diagnosis, Bro and I both left Queensland and went to be with him in Sydney. I drove mine and Chumpy's van – the one he left his wallet and phone in the day he went spearfishing – with Rummi beside me. The van didn't have Bluetooth, so I played Chumpy's Love Charli CD, singing along at the top of my lungs and crying harder than I've ever cried. There were only eight songs and I played them on repeat, over and over again. The words became a loop in my mind.

Every inch of the drive between the Gold Coast and Sydney was a reminder of what was. Chumpy and I did many trips along the east coast in our van. We'd sleep on the mattress in the back, survive on Vegemite and cheese jaffles, and listen to music nonstop. We'd stop off at Woolgoolga, Sawtell and Arrawarra Headland, where Chumpy went camping as a kid. Every turn-off sign was a trigger. Driving in the van was the loneliest I've ever felt.

Our last trip together was in February 2020, when Chumpy and I drove down to see my dad, Em in Wollongong and Chris and Sally in Eden. We were only meant to stay with Em for a night, but we ended up spending a few days with her. We went surfing every morning and Chump and Em and her then-partner, Jordy, jammed together – Chumpy on the guitar, Em on the drums – like the good old days.

That visit was the last time Em saw her brother. Sometimes it feels like he knew; that's why he stayed two extra nights with Em, and why he came back to hug his parents on the dock, and me in the garage.

When I pulled into my dad's driveway in Warriewood, he looked surprisingly normal. He'd just had a surgery to remove part of the tumour from his brain, and that bought him some time and relief. 'I feel like I can think again,' he explained. 'It's like the pressure in my brain has eased.'

It was a temporary relief. No matter how much we wished it wasn't, Dad's cancer was terminal. Holding out for a miracle, I booked in for a consultation with renowned neurosurgeon Doctor Charlie Teo. His assessment was black and white. There was no sugar-coating it. I recorded what Dr Teo said, with his permission.

'Look, Pete, you're sixty-eight. You've had a great life,' he said with the straightforwardness of someone who has to deliver shit news every day. 'We could do this radical surgery – which will cost $150,000 – to remove a portion of your brain, but you would lose your eyesight and risk your memory, and we wouldn't be able to guarantee that it would give you any more time. You *might* live a bit longer, but we don't know how much you'd lose.

'Because the cancer is stage four, there are two really bad options, and both of them result in you dying. If I do the operation, you are still going to die. If I don't do the operation, you are still going to die, but maybe a bit sooner. They are essentially the same option.'

The prognosis was utterly devastating.

When we left the appointment, I was bawling my eyes out. Dad was silent. I'd never seen him so quiet. I don't know if Dad was trying to protect me or if he was in complete shock, but he fought back his tears. His mouth didn't move, but he looked at me and his eyes asked, 'What do you think we should do?' I didn't have an answer for him. We called Bro to fill him in and then sat in silence.

It was a decision only Dad could make, and he made it right away. 'I'm not getting that surgery,' he declared. That was that. What was the point of living if he couldn't surf or ride his motorbike or see his kids' faces? It was Dad's choice and we respected it.

Dad stared down his fate: he understood that he wasn't going to survive stage four brain cancer. Even if he was the Northern Beaches' Crocodile Dundee, he wasn't invincible. It must have been a terrifying realisation, but he approached his radiation therapy with the same childlike awe with which he lived his whole life. 'I feel like a little rat in a science experiment. I'm excited to see what happens and where this is going to go,' he'd say.

'It's not going anywhere good, Dad,' I'd reply, sharing his dark sense of humour.

As much as it hurt, it wasn't a huge surprise to me and Bro; Dad's mortality had been sitting at the edge of our vision for some time. He'd had two heart attacks already and had been diagnosed with the heart condition Wolff-Parkinson-White syndrome. His own father had died of a stroke. It's natural to worry about your parents dying, and while we knew one day we'd lose our dad, we never guessed it would be brain cancer and so soon.

For as long as I can remember, Dad always went on about his will. He would call me out of the blue to make sure I knew his will was in his top drawer and to remind me that Bro was the executor. Maybe it was because he'd survived two heart attacks, but Dad was especially aware of his mortality. He figured he'd be out surfing, riding his motorbike or doing something that he loved – because he was never not doing something that he loved – and bang, he'd be gone. That was the way Chumpy went out, but it wasn't the same for my dad. We lost him piece by piece.

My brother and I moved back into our childhood bedrooms at Dad's house. Nothing ever changed at Dad's place. The same curtains I peered out of as a kid were hanging over my bedroom window. My cupboard was filled with the toys and junk of my childhood, and Bro's bed was made of a mattress on top of milk crates. Dad's house was a time warp, a maze of memories and a treasure chest – if you count clutter as treasure. There's a running joke in our family that one of Bro's girlfriends left a yoga mat stretched out in the hallway one day and it became Dad's new rug. It stayed there for years, just like the mug I put down on the coffee table and the old bill Dad stuck to the fridge.

For three months, I slept in my old bedroom and took Dad to all of his appointments, scans and radiation therapy sessions. Even though he decided against having the radical neurosurgery, we were still doing whatever we could to slow the cancer growth and buy him whatever time possible. At the appointments, the doctors would often address questions to me because Dad wasn't quite with it.

'Has Pete had any headaches?' they'd ask.

'Nah, I'm feeling great,' Dad would answer.

'Dad, you literally had a massive migraine yesterday,' I'd chime in.

The questions were basic, but they spoke volumes. What day is it? Can you order your own coffee at the café? Who drove here? Dad would answer all the questions with such sincerity. He genuinely believed he'd driven us to the hospital when, actually, I had.

The doctors explained that glioblastoma affects the patient's cognitive functioning and memory loss is a common symptom. Dad handled it all like a trooper and chose to find the humour and silver linings in every moment. We followed his lead and made light of his mistakes. If Dad could laugh about it, so could we.

Dad also started eating copious amounts of fresh garlic and ginger because a friend told him it helped with inflammation. He absolutely stank. Every day, Bro and I would have the same hilarious battle with him. 'Dad, you stink. Can you please put your shirt in the wash and have a shower?'

'This is a new shirt,' he'd say.

'You've been wearing it for five days.'

Even though we joked about the stench, we never let Dad miss his dose of garlic and ginger. He'd bring containers with chopped up garlic and ginger everywhere we went. On days he felt well, Bro and I would take Dad to his favourite place: Terrey Hills Tavern.

'Do you guys want to share a plate of nachos?' he'd ask.

'Sounds good,' we'd say, only to watch him pour a mountain of garlic and ginger on top, making it basically inedible to us. 'God, Dad, you could just put it on your side!'

Dad's cancer was never an elephant in the room. We talked about it openly and made – frankly – quite dark jokes. That was Dad's way. I asked him if he wanted to make a bucket list, but he just wanted to do what he always did: go to the beach, take his motorbike for a spin and go to the pub up the road for 2 for 1 steak night.

'Dad, you literally have weeks to live. Let's go out and order oysters instead of the cheap steak night,' I'd suggest, but he wasn't having a bar of it. Dad always bought home-brand products, he'd never splurge on an expensive meal and he swore by the public school and hospital systems. He wasn't poor, but he lived a thrifty life, and he stayed almost entirely himself. Almost.

The hardest thing for Dad was losing the freedom of his motorbike. The friends he rode with were worried about how wobbly he was getting. 'The boys don't want me riding with them anymore,' Dad told me with such sadness in his voice. 'They don't want to be responsible for me.'

Dad never rode his beloved motorbike again.

It was crushing to see Dad upset, but I like to think he found comfort in Rummi. He fell in absolute love with her. Even though Dad always had rescued possums, birds and lizards living in and outside his house, he wasn't a fan of domesticated animals. He thought they should be free and wild. But that all changed when we were staying with him. Rummi was so in tune with him. Whenever he sat on the couch, she'd curl up next to him and they'd cuddle together, all cosy and cute.

Seeing Rummi spending such precious time with Dad made me think about the time with Chumpy that was stolen from her too. I put my heartache over Chumpy to the side to focus on Dad, but when I had a moment to myself to think about what I'd lost and what I was about to lose, I fell apart.

People ask me how I coped after Chumpy died. I didn't. Before I left for Sydney, I threw a massive party for Chumpy's birthday on 20 September. We celebrated like he was still alive. We printed off photos of Chumpy's face and wore them as masks, along with his hats, beanies and Red Bull helmet. My friend made a gluten-free carrot cake with the number thirty-three on it, and we sang Happy Birthday, screaming, 'Happy birthday, Chumppppyyyyy! Where the bloody hell are ya?' He wasn't there to blow out his candles, so we did it for him. Bro made a speech and I thanked everyone for coming, and in that moment, we all remembered he wasn't there, and why. It was the biggest headfuck. It was so emotional – there were a lot of drunken tears. It felt wrong to be having a party without him, but it would have been even worse not to mark the day. It was a catch-22.

The very next day, I drove down to Sydney to be with my dad. When I got there, I kept getting caught in the same catch-22: I didn't want to have fun without Chumpy, but I desperately needed any kind of distraction to take my mind off Chumpy. I'd go out to dinner with our mutual friends to try to cheer myself up, but the sight of the empty chair next to me would break my heart. Why are tables designed to fit even numbers? I hated being the odd number.

The numbness I'd felt in the early days was wearing off and I couldn't cope with the pain left in its wake. I started rebelling like an angsty teenager, except I was rebelling against the world instead of my parents, because I was twenty-eight. Every night, I'd go out and party with my friends, and every morning I'd wake up with a slight hangover to take Dad to his appointments. I don't know if my friends were grieving Chump too, if they were trying to support me in whatever way I needed, or if they had their own things going on, but we all wanted to party. It was obvious that we were drinking away our sorrows, and I started to understand how alcoholics became so – the relief of numbness was addictive. Not that I ever thought I was an alcoholic. I was a young widow, missing the love of my life and turning to my friends for comfort. I don't know if it makes me a bad person, but I genuinely had fun on my nights out in Sydney. We'd drink and dance, sing and cry. It was cathartic. I felt like I was unleashing my sorrow, even if it was only a momentary release. Pain relief came when I was belting out Tracy Chapman hits at the local pizza joint in Avalon well past closing time. It came when I was choreographing daggy dance routines with my girls. And it came after the third margarita.

Chumpy hated smoking with a passion and I never got into it, not least because it made me cough and splutter like a total rookie. But I remember going out in Sydney one night and puffing on my friends' vape pens. I knew Chump would hate it – and the next day, I hated myself for it – but that night, he wasn't there, so who gave a shit! I knew vaping wasn't going to kill me – it is probably the lamest form of rebellion – but that night, I really had a 'fuck life' attitude.

And, deep down, I was probably hoping that if I choked on enough vapes, Chumpy would come back and tell me off for being silly.

It's almost ironic that the thing that saved me during those months in Sydney was the ocean – the same ocean that took Chumpy from me. I would walk Rummi at the beach every morning and took to jumping into the sea, diving under the waves. He told me to find him at the bottom of the sea and my god, I searched for him. I still do.

'Fuuuckkkk,' I'd yell under the water where no-one could hear me – except, maybe, Chumpy.

These days I don't scream as much anymore. I just open my eyes when I dive under waves and say, 'Hi Chump.'

CHAPTER ELEVEN

For You

I was afraid Chris and Sally couldn't see a light out of the darkness of their grief. I felt a kind of responsibility to remind them there was good in the world. They were my family, and family sticks together. While I was in Sydney, I invited them and Em to come and stay with me at a friend's holiday house in Avalon. It was a beautiful sandstone home with views overlooking Pittwater. Chumpy would've loved it.

Surrounded by the beauty of the bay, I could see Chris and Sal were being suffocated by sadness. I looked at Rummi and thought about how much comfort and love she gave me, and decided that's exactly what they needed: a kelpie. I started campaigning for them to get a dog and trawling Gumtree for puppy listings. Chris was quite particular – he loved Rummi, and knew how much Chump loved Rummi, so he wanted a dog exactly like her. She had to be a pure kelpie with the same markings and affectionate personality.

The very next week, Stella came tearing into their lives, full of energy and licks. She and Rummi got on like best buddies and it felt like another connection to Chump; like the axe he and Chris made together, the songs they used to sing in the car as a family and the guitar his mum gave him.

A couple of months later, I booked a stay in a little beach shack at Kiama for me, Chris, Sally and Emma – and Rummi and Stella, of course. I woke up before everyone else one morning and took Rummi for a walk as the sun was coming up. I was sitting on the beach when I got the Instagram DM. It was from my friend Fisher's manager, who lived in the United States.

Hey, this guy I know from London just died. This is his partner's page, can you connect with her?

She was a pretty blonde woman named Lotte Bowser, who taught yoga and loved music. She was also a writer. Lotte's fiancé's name was Ben and when I first saw a photo of him, I did a double-take. He looked eerily like Chumpy, with long hair, beautiful olive skin and eyes that told a story.

Ben's story was a brutal one. In 2019, he was diagnosed with Malignant Peripheral Nerve Sheath Tumour, a very rare and aggressive type of cancer. He was thirty-five. After undergoing surgery and six weeks of radiation therapy, a routine scan on the day after his thirty-sixth birthday found multiple tumours in his lungs. Ben's cancer had metastasised and the doctors told him it was stage four – terminal.

'We're very sorry, but this isn't something we're able to cure,' the doctors said. 'The cancer will eventually kill you.'

The prognosis hit Ben and Lotte like a grenade. The health system had put their hands in the air and said there was nothing more they could do. Ben was told to go home and get his affairs in order – basically, go home and prepare to die. After the initial shock wore off, they simply refused to accept that their time was up. 'I am simply too young to accept this prognosis, and I will not give up,' Ben wrote at the time.

In the September of 2020 – two months after I lost Chump – Ben and Lotte travelled to Tijuana, Mexico so he could start a different form of treatment there. The initial results were positive – Ben's tumours either stayed the same size, shrank or disappeared. Lotte started looking forward to the day when Ben would be cancer-free, but before that day could come, Ben caught Covid-19. He spent twenty-four days on a ventilator – separated from Lotte, who was forced to quarantine alone in a foreign country. The last time Lotte saw Ben alive and conscious, he was lying on a hospital stretcher with a tube down his mouth. She had to wear a hazmat suit, two pairs of gloves and plastic bags covering her shoes. She couldn't hug Ben or kiss him goodbye.

On 14 November 2020, Ben died of multiple organ failure as a result of complications from Covid-19 and cancer. He was alone. So was Lotte.

As I read Lotte's story, I felt every inch of her pain. In her Instagram post announcing Ben's passing, she described the exact void I was still feeling:

Friends – Our beautiful Ben left his physical body last night, 14.11.2020. The day my world turned black and life changed forever...

I can't believe I am even writing this. I know how many of you loved him and I'm hurting for all of us so much right now. He will never be replaced and this void will never heal.

Finding Lotte was a revelation – I wasn't alone in losing my soulmate far too young. Lotte was a widow, just like me. I hadn't connected with anyone going through the same thing as me until then.

I can't remember how long I sat on the beach at Kiama, looking at Lotte's Instagram, but I do remember running back to the beach shack to tell Chris and Sally that I wasn't the only young widow in the world.

'Guys, there's this girl in London who's in my position right now. She's just lost her person as well. I'm not alone,' I said, showing them a picture of Lotte and Ben.

Lotte's story was so sad, but in a weird way, it gave me some kind of comfort. Is that bad to admit? I was relieved to have found someone to talk to who understood what I was going through. We might have been on opposite sides of the planet, but we were walking in each other's – very painful and unwanted – shoes.

As soon as we started messaging each other on Instagram, Lotte and I clicked. It was like we were destined. There was a nine-hour time difference and 16,994 kilometres between us, but some days, Lotte was the closest person in the world to me. Our friendship grew from Instagram messages to WhatsApp conversations to voice notes then video messages and eventually video calls. We spoke every day, sometimes for hours. We'd have long conversations at all hours of the night and day, pouring our hearts out to each other, telling stories about our boys and laughing at morbid jokes we couldn't tell in front of anyone else. If we didn't laugh, we'd cry.

I would often speak to Lotte early in the morning – her night-time – as I was walking Rummi at the beach in the sunshine, while she was stuck inside her apartment in grey, locked-down London. I felt a fair amount of guilt that I was able to process my grief freely, to tap into the healing powers of the ocean and hug my friends, while Lotte was by herself. She described the experience as 'PTSD without the P' – so just Traumatic Stress Disorder. It was so unfair.

It's hard for me to admit, but some days, Lotte's grief felt too raw, too inescapable, too enormous for me to take on. Some days, my own grief was all I could carry. Some days, I had to be selfish and tap out just to survive.

Most of the time, though, Lotte and I leaned on each other. There was something about Lotte that reminded me so much of Chumpy. They have the same essence. They're both super wise, articulate and have an ease about them.

When Lotte tells me about Ben, often she could be talking about Chumpy. They were similar in so many ways and if they'd met in this world, they would have definitely been friends. We like to think they've met in another world and have guided us towards each other. This might sound woo-woo, but we both think Chumpy and Ben brought us together, orchestrating our friendship from above.

After Ben died, Lotte went to see a clairvoyant. 'I'm getting signs from ... Alex,' the psychic said. 'Do you know an Alex?'

Lotte shook her head no, she didn't know anyone called Alex. It wasn't until a few days later that she remembered Chumpy's real name.

After we did a couple of Instagram Live videos together, talking about our shared experiences, Lotte and I realised how many people connected with our stories. Lotte was the first widow I met when I felt like I was in a tragic club of one but, since then, I've gotten hundreds of messages from hundreds of other women just like me. Loss doesn't discriminate; it can hit any one of us at any time. Everyone is fighting their own battle. Everyone goes through shit. No one knows exactly what someone is dealing with behind closed doors or inside their mind. I'm certainly not special because my partner died.

If I could cancel my membership to the widows' club, I would do it in a heartbeat, obviously, but considering that wasn't an option for either of us, Lotte wanted to pour herself into something positive. She has a gift with words, so we decided to write a grief handbook together to share our hard-learned lessons. The result was *Now What? A Guide to Navigating Life After Loss*. It's something we both wish we could have had when we were totally lost in the aftermath of our losses. We were the first to admit we weren't experts on the subject, but we thought there was space for our real, messy and relatable lived experiences.

More than anything, I wanted to make it clear that there isn't one correct way to grieve. Grief isn't linear. The five stages of grief – denial, anger, bargaining, depression and acceptance – don't always happen in that order. Grief is a clusterfuck of emotions. I've felt rage then hope, followed by loneliness and guilt – sometimes in the space of a single morning. There's no one-size-fits-all solution. That's something I wish I'd known sooner, especially when I genuinely thought I was a sociopath because I didn't realise I was in shock.

As much as our workbook is for people who've lost someone, it's also for that person's loved ones who want to better support them and understand what they're going through. We wanted to normalise talking about grief, acknowledging it for what it is and not making it the elephant in the room. When someone dies, it can often be hard to talk about them, but it's even harder not talking about them, or pretending they didn't exist or that they aren't desperately missed. The worst thing I can imagine is Chumpy being forgotten. I love talking about him and hearing stories from other people; I'd hate to think someone was afraid to bring him up in conversation with me.

I also can't stand the feeling of being coddled or treated like a child. When Chumpy first died, all I wanted was to be treated like a normal person instead of a fragile glass ornament that could break at any second (even though I was). I didn't want to be smothered, and I actually had to tell some people to back up because I felt like they were suffocating me and it was driving me away. I also didn't want to be given any special treatment just because I was going through some hectic shit. I couldn't stand it when my mates were overly nice to me and felt like they couldn't act like we usually did, mucking around and taking the piss out of me.

Obviously, everyone is different – that's the main message in our workbook – but I'm pretty sure no-one enjoys having people walk on eggshells around them. When I met Lotte, I think that's what I appreciated most about her – I could say anything and even if she couldn't relate to it, she got it. She didn't shy away from the messiness of what we were both going through.

It's pretty wild that Lotte and I haven't met in person yet. We've known each other for almost two years – shared our darkest days, thoughts and tears – but we haven't hugged. When that moment happens, it'll be beautiful. As much as I'm grateful to have Lotte in my life, I wish it were under different circumstances. For us both.

Lotte said something in the early days of our friendship that has stuck with me ever since: 'If not with you, then for you.'

If I couldn't live with Chumpy, I'd live for him, I vowed.

The first song Chump learned to play on the guitar on his own was 'Little Wing' by Jimi Hendrix, who was probably his most favourite musician of all time. He had the song title tattooed on his inner right forearm. The month after he passed, I got the exact same tattoo.

Fly on.

CHAPTER TWELVE

The Turn-off to Minnie Waters

I don't know how, but time seemed to go slow and race by at the same time. Everything was happening, and nothing was happening. While my father was slipping through my fingers and the reality of Chumpy being gone was sinking in, Chumpy's sperm sample still sat on the shelf above my grief. Knowing it was there was a glimmer a hope – a chance of new life amidst all the death. I knew exactly where the shelf was in my mind, but it took me six months before I could actually reach for it.

I'd made the decision during the three months I was living with Dad, but it became real on the drive from Sydney back to the Gold Coast in December 2020. Dad was stable and it looked like he was going to defy the doctors and live into the New Year, so I took the opportunity to go home: to my home, to Chump's home. I felt like I'd ignored my reality for as long as I could and I needed to face up to it. I had to be in my own space, with my own thoughts, between my own sheets rather than the old doona cover of my childhood.

To break up the trip, I stayed with my friend Ash in Newcastle. Ash had given birth to her daughter Oceanna, her second child, exactly a month after Chumpy died. She had a waterbirth and named me Oceanna's godmother.

I was holding Oceanna the morning I was supposed to leave Newcastle and keep driving north when I heard the opening bars of Chumpy's song 'Four Babies', which is actually about the four strings on his ukulele. I thought Ash must have been playing it in the kitchen and I was quietly chuffed to hear someone else listening to his songs. When Ash came out of the kitchen, she asked me where the music was coming from – she hadn't been playing it. For a second, we both thought we were imagining things. I handed Oceanna to Ash and grabbed my bags to take them to the van.

As soon as we stepped outside, we realised the music was coming from inside the van – our rundown old van with its shitty CD player that barely worked when the car was on. The van was off and had been parked in the same spot all night, but I kid you not, it was playing Chumpy's song 'Four Babies'. When I unlocked and opened the door, the music blasted out. Both me and Ash had tears in our eyes and our mouths were wide open. We couldn't believe it. Even now writing it down, it seems totally impossible, but it happened; we filmed it because it was so surreal.

I couldn't wait to hit the road that day because I knew Chump was going to be with me. Unlike the drive down to Sydney, I didn't feel painfully alone. The drive up to the Gold Coast was such a therapeutic trip. It was on this drive that I knew I was going to have Chumpy's baby.

I'd made the decision before I left Sydney that when I got home, I would start the IVF journey, but it wasn't until the drive that my decision became real. I was driving past Arrawarra, where Chumpy and I always used to stop on our trips, when I saw the turn-off sign to Minnie Waters. I was captivated by it. Everything became clear: I was going to have a baby and if she was a girl, I was going to call her Minnie Alex.

As it happened, the day I left Newcastle was the day I was scheduled to have a phone interview with an IVF counsellor to make sure I was of sound mind before starting the process. The conversation happened on the side of the Pacific Highway.

'Why do you want to do this on your own?' the counsellor asked.

'This is what Chumpy would have wanted – and it's also what I want. We were always going to start a family together and I'm ready to do it,' I said. 'I want to carry on his legacy and bring his baby into the world.'

'How are you going to manage being a single parent and raising the child without him?'

'Of course, it's not going to be a walk in the park. I know that. There will be hard days, but I'm prepared for them, and I'm lucky to have a great support network around me, including my mum, brother and close friends.'

'Are you going to tell the child about their father?'

'I'll tell the baby about their dad from day dot. I'll play his music at home and tell stories about him every night before bed.'

'So, what will you say when the child asks where their dad is?'

'They won't need to. The kid will know everything about their dad. There won't be any confusion. They will know their daddy is in the sky.'

'How will you cope with the constant reminder of your loss?'

'I know having a baby will accentuate parts of my grief, especially when we mark milestones without Chumpy, but having the baby will outweigh all of that.' I'd thought about it a lot. 'I'm choosing to do this without Chumpy; it's wild that I'm having to make this choice, but this is what I want.'

When the call ended, I felt like I'd answered all of the counsellor's questions and ticked her boxes. The conversation really cemented in my mind that I'd thought things through and knew what I was getting myself into.

Of course, I wished more than anything that I didn't have to consider the realities of being a single parent, but that option had been taken away from me. I had no control over it. I could only control what happened next.

When we got home after three months away, Rummi ran through the house, sniffing and searching from room to room. She was looking for Chumpy. It broke my heart.

'Sorry, Rum-Dog. It's just us,' I told her.

The house was exactly how we left it. Chumpy's clothes were still in our wardrobe. They still are. His to-do list was still pinned to the corkboard in the walk-in pantry. It still is. And his electric toothbrush was still on our bathroom vanity. I still use it. I moved his toiletries – deodorant, razor and Issey Miyake fragrance – from the bathroom bench to the cupboard under the sink. On his side of the sink where he would brush his teeth in the morning hangs a cross-stitch of a line from Bon Iver's 'Skinny Love' that he used to sing all the time. It is about being a different kind of here.

As much as everything was the same, it was completely different. Chumpy was everywhere and nowhere.

I still felt closest to Chumpy in his music room, surrounded by his guitars and all the cords and pedals he had perfectly organised in a way that made sense only to him.

There's a fine line between keeping a shrine and holding on to memories. Some things were easy for me to let go of. Chumpy's dad kept the axe they made together, his sister took some of his old jackets and my brother uses his GoPro camera and jetski, while some of his best friends ride his beloved surfboards. Other things I haven't been able to part with, like his hats, journals and laptop, which I've started using. When I sign into a Zoom meeting now, the name still comes up as Alex Pullin.

The practical things were the hardest to deal with. What was I meant to do with Chumpy's phone? It was basically brand-new. I didn't want to use it myself, but I certainly didn't want to chuck it out or sell it. I ended up giving it to Em. She didn't do a factory reset on it, so now she gets daily memories pop up of whatever me and Chumpy were doing years ago, which is both beautiful and brutal.

It's the memories that keep us going, but also what hurt the most. In Chumpy's bedside table at his parents' house, Em found a zine she made for his twenty-fifth birthday when she was too broke to afford a present. Each page had a drawing and a memory.

When Chumpy was two, he held his breath for three minutes

When Chumpy was three, he rode down the stairs on a plastic bike

When Chumpy was thirteen, he started a punk band

When Chumpy was fourteen, he chose to be a professional snowboarder

When Chumpy was eighteen, he became a folk singer

When Chumpy was twenty-four, he won the crystal globe

When Chumpy was twenty-five, he became an extreme sports calendar model

I think Em was taking the piss with that last one – it was accompanied by a very realistic drawing of Chump posing topless – that made him and everyone laugh.

My period was due the week I got back to the Gold Coast, so I booked in to see my IVF doctor. Mum came to every single appointment with me. She was there for me every step of the way, holding my hand and being my rock. Her presence gave me strength. Mum didn't question me or try to make decisions for me, she just supported me.

The first step in the IVF process is stimulating the follicles in the ovaries to encourage them to produce more eggs. For two weeks, I injected myself with hormones to do just that. Some women have intense side effects from the injections including nausea, mood swings, anxiety and fatigue. I was lucky I didn't notice anything much different to regular PMS. Honestly, dealing with hormonal imbalances was the least of my problems.

After twelve days of needles, I went in for the egg retrieval. I wasn't afraid. I didn't want to be put under, though – I hate being knocked out – so the doctor gave me the green whistle with the happy gas and worked his magic while I was conscious. I laughed the entire time, feeling like I was ten margaritas deep. I remember talking to Chump, cheering out, 'Come on, Chump, let's get these eggs!'

At one point, the doctor had to tell me to stop laughing because I was moving around too much. There's probably a good reason why they put people under anaesthetic, hey?

Despite my fits of giggles, we ended up with eight embryos. Of those, only three survived. Three little miracles. I didn't waste any time. I had the first embryo inserted before the end of the month.

Of course, Mum came with me to the appointment and sat beside me as I held my legs up in the air. After the transfer, I remember sitting in the car with Mum desperately trying not to sneeze – I didn't want the embryo to fall out of me! I was pulling faces and laughing, and Mum was shaking her head and laughing with me. 'Do you think it fell out?' I asked when the sneeze snuck out.

'No, I don't think it fell out, Ellidy,' she assured me.

Mum spent so much time looking after me, I think her own grief got pushed to the side. I was in my own world, so I didn't give much thought to what my mum was going through. She'd lost someone too. Mum loved Chump like her own son. It must have been heartbreaking for her to know that Chumpy was gone, and so too was our future together. None of it was easy.

After the transfer, I steeled myself to start the new year without Chumpy. It was going to be my first New Year's Day alone in eight years. I was dreading the thought of not following our tradition of perching on a rock overlooking the ocean with a bottle of champagne and Chumpy's guitar. So I packed up the van – with Rummi beside me and the embryo in my tummy – and made my way to Hat Head in New South Wales to spend New Year's Eve with my friend Ash and her family at their beach shack.

We were getting ready to go to the shack next door for a party when I went to the bathroom and found I was bleeding. I knew exactly what was happening: the embryo hadn't implanted. I was losing this little baby.

I didn't want to ruin the night for everyone else, so I didn't say anything. At the party, I listened to the music and forced a smile. Ash picked up that something was wrong but didn't press me on it. The truth was, I just needed to hold it together for the night and allow myself time to think it through privately.

The next morning, I was a fucking mess. Everyone was wishing each other a happy new year, but there was nothing happy about it. I couldn't understand how we were entering a new year without Chumpy. How could time still be ticking by? I didn't want to leave him behind, I didn't want to say, 'Chumpy died *last* year.' I wanted to stay in 2020 because that was the last year he'd known. The more time passed, the further away Chumpy got.

Another of our friends, Bella, and her family, joined me and Ash at the beach shack. It was such a wholesome family day, and I was all alone. I'd lost Chumpy and our baby. I loved my mates and their families – and I wasn't jealous or resentful of their happiness – but they were a stark reminder of what I didn't have.

I was surrounded by two close friends, their loving partners and their adorable babies, and I was utterly miserable. I was watching the little kids run around when I told Ash and Bella about the bleeding. 'I know that it was the bub coming out,' I said, bawling my eyes out.

I called Lizzo later that day to tell her what had happened.

'I lost the baby,' I said.

There was silence for a moment as she tried to find the words to comfort me. But she had something to tell me too.

'I'm pregnant,' she said a little later. She'd only just found out and it was the best news.

I realised how hard it was for her to tell me. I was beyond happy for Lizzo and so glad she told me, sad for myself and a bit lost in the world.

Losing the baby struck a fear I'd never known inside me. I knew that only one per cent of Chumpy's sperm was viable, but I had been certain that that was going to be enough. Maybe I was wrong. Maybe we hadn't retrieved the sperm in time, maybe my eggs weren't any good, maybe the IVF wasn't going to work at all.

I'd promised myself that I wouldn't do endless rounds of IVF. As much as I wanted to have our baby – and as much as I'd done everything I could to make that a reality – it was in the hands of the universe. I knew I couldn't have kept facing loss after loss, and I really couldn't afford to keep trying more than the three embryos we'd collected. I'd paid for my first round of IVF, which was around $8000 after the rebates, Mum had offered to pay for the second, and Chumpy's parents put their hands up for the third. I had two more shots. If it was meant to be, it would be.

I wanted to insert the second embryo straightaway, but the doctor convinced me to wait a month. I'd had a blood test and my hormone levels weren't too good. I didn't want to wait a minute longer, I wanted to rip in and get on with it. I didn't want to sit around, wasting time and thinking about worst-case scenarios. Those embryos were the only things keeping me going, and the thought of losing that hope was too painful to bear.

Even so, I did as I was told and waited a month before doing my second embryo transfer. I was on the clinic table, with my mum holding my hand beside me and the doctor between my legs. There was a sheet over my legs, so I didn't see the doctor stick the tube inside me, but I felt it. As I was lying there, I had a vision: *it's a girl*.

I knew I was pregnant. I *knew* it. This one was going to stick.

My friends kept telling me to do a pregnancy test, but I didn't need to. I waited for two weeks to get a blood test from my doctor, and they called me as soon as the results came in. 'Congratulations, Ellidy, the test came back positive. You're pregnant.'

It was six months after Chumpy died, and I was pregnant.

The first person I told, naturally, was Rummi. 'You're going to be a big sister,' I squealed. Mum was still living with me at that point, so she heard the good news too. When I video-called Chumpy's parents, we all burst into tears. They were going to be grandparents. I was going to be a mum. We were going to have Chumpy's baby.

When I was ten weeks along, I went down to Eden. I picked Emma up along the way and we drove down together in the van. She was stoked for me, even though I kept having to pull over every half-an-hour or so to vomit on the side of the road. I was too early to be showing any signs of a bump, and if I hadn't been so sick and tired, I would've been in denial that I was pregnant. I already found it hard to believe. I didn't have a belly or a husband, but I was having a baby. Maybe seeing Chumpy's parents when I was pregnant would make it feel real. That's what I was hoping, anyway.

On our drive down, Rummi sat in the back of the van, with Chumpy's ashes in a box next to her. When I'd been given the ashes after the funeral and formalities, I was shocked by how heavy they were. I thought they'd be light as a feather, like ashes from a fire, but they landed in my hands with a thud. We didn't want a pretty urn for Chump. I didn't want an urn at all. Fuck, I wanted a walking, talking Chump. Not an urn. So they put him in a thick wooden box. I didn't really know what to do with them. For six months, the box had sat in Chumpy's music studio. I figured I'd bring them down on my visit to Chumpy's parents and we could decide what to do with them together. I imagined us doing some meaningful ceremony at their local beach and releasing Chumpy into the sea, his favourite place. It didn't happen that trip. Chumpy's ashes are still at his parent's place. We can't bring ourselves to do anything with them yet.

Visiting Eden is always very emotional for me. I look around the dinner table at the four chairs and think, 'It should be Chumpy here, not me. Why isn't Chumpy here?' The Pullins were such a close family of four and not having Chumpy there felt all wrong. I would've given anything to trade places with Chumpy so his family could have him back.

But the reality was that they were stuck with me. I don't know if it helped or hurt having me around, reminding them of Chumpy. I like to think it was the former.

Em always says she feels Chumpy the strongest when we're both together, like he's there with us. 'Because where else would he fucking be?'

I know you're 'meant' to wait until the twelve-week mark, but I told my close friends I was pregnant the same day I found out. They'd all been there for me during the dark days, and I wanted them to be a part of the bright ones too. In a way, it was almost a relief to talk – and think – about something other than my loss. I loved talking about Chumpy, sharing memories and listening to his music with other people, but sometimes it felt like those conversations made the void bigger.

There were days when all I wanted to do was scroll through photos and watch videos of Chumpy and me together. Other times, I couldn't bear to hear the sound of his voice on his songs. Sometimes I needed to look at his face, and others I couldn't stand to. Even now, I find it hard to listen to certain songs – including 'Falling,' the track he wrote for my twenty-first birthday – without falling into a heap.

There wasn't time for that – I was growing a baby.

The first trimester hit me hard. I was nauseous, lethargic and so damn tired all the time. I immediately thought of Lizzo. I even rang her to apologise because in the early days of her pregnancy I thought she was being withdrawn and maybe distancing herself from me. 'I'm so sorry, I didn't realise how shocking you must have been feeling,' I said. 'I get it now.'

I got quite good at having a sly spew. Sometimes, when I walked Rummi at the beach of a morning, I'd have to lean over into the water to throw up. More often, though, the nausea would hit when I was driving back home from the beach. In those (very frequent) instances, I would reach for one of Rummi's poo bags and do what needed to be done. They weren't my classiest moments, but I was so pumped to be pregnant I kinda found the symptoms funny. Plus, spewing always makes you feel better.

All my friends told me they thought I was having a boy – a mini Alex – but I knew from the moment I lay down on the IVF clinic table that I was having a little girl. I didn't find out before the birth because I wanted it to be a surprise. Regardless of whether the baby was a boy or a girl, they were a fucking miracle.

I told my dad the happy news over the phone the day I found out, but I wasn't sure if it sank in. I so wanted him to be a part of the baby's life, so I booked a surprise trip to Sydney to show him my tiny bump. I pulled a classic Elli-copter move and got a friend to pick me up from the airport and take me to Dad's so I could scare him. The fright soon turned to joy. 'I'm pregnant, Dad, I'm having a baby,' I said, pulling him into a big hug.

It was surreal to think this baby was created out of Chumpy's death and growing while my dad was dying. Dad always joked, 'out with the old, in with the new'. How fucking morbid. I tried not to think about that, and focused on the sweetness of new life, instead of the bitterness of good men taken too soon.

During my pregnancy, I became a chip monster. I survived almost entirely on hot chips, so much so that people would message me with their recommendations of the best chips in town.

'Have you tried the chips at the fish shop at Tugun? They're bloody good, but you need to ask for extra chicken salt,' the hot chip hot tips would say.

I became a connoisseur of chippies, and discovered the delights of KFC chips for the first time in my life. Up until then I was typically a Maccas girl. One afternoon when

I was licking the chicken salt from my fingers, I remembered the conversation I had with Chumpy about how I was going to be only eating healthy foods when I was pregnant. Chumpy would be looking down laughing at me.

My chip obsession was so great, it influenced my baby name ideas. I was watching TV with my brother a few days before my due date, and I heard someone say the word 'chipper'.

'That's it!' I thought.

'I love that,' I said to Bro. 'I think I want to change the baby's name to Chippa Chumpy Pullin, if it's a boy.'

The next day, I called Emma to check in. 'How are you going?' I asked, bracing myself because I knew she was having a tough time.

'I've actually been quite chipper,' she said.

I gasped. 'I can't believe you just said that word, Em! Who says chipper? It's so weird,' I said, explaining my change to the boy name. She loved it.

I wasn't sure how and when I was going to announce my pregnancy publicly. It still felt quite unbelievable to me, so I didn't know how other people would react to the news that I was having my late partner's baby. In the end, my hand was pushed. My management had a call from a television station, asking for a comment on the whispers they'd heard that I was pregnant with Chumpy's child.

We responded with the standard, 'No comment,' but I knew I had to say something soon if I wanted to make the announcement on my own terms.

I waited until I was twenty-four weeks pregnant, and my belly was well and truly showing, to announce the pregnancy to the world. Part of me was afraid. I didn't want to jinx the pregnancy and risk a miscarriage by saying it out loud. I was also worried if I made the announcement before I had a decent baby bump, people would think I was losing the plot.

'Oh, look at that poor widow, she thinks she's pregnant, but her partner died almost a year ago, it's impossible,' I imagined them saying.

Worse still, I was conscious that some people wouldn't agree with my decision. I know in some circles, IVF is frowned upon – even more so when it's done using sperm from someone who's passed away. It's not the 'done thing'.

'How can you do that? He's dead, he's not here to consent, it's wrong.' I didn't want to hear any negative judgements.

Of course, in an ideal world, a child would have two parents. Newsflash: we don't live in an ideal world. To those who thought it was selfish of me to bring a baby into the world without their dad, I point to all the single mothers who've gone before me – either by choice or necessity – and raised good people. I nod to the divorce rate and the generations of kids who grew up in broken families – myself included. I think of the mothers who've become widows while pregnant, which could have been me. When Chumpy died, there was a chance we could have conceived in the days and weeks before. We all clung on to that chance until my period came and dashed the hope.

I knew people were going to question how I'd become pregnant with Chumpy's baby, and I wasn't going to lie about it. I was completely and utterly confident in my choice and didn't feel any shame about having the baby Chumpy and I so desperately wanted. I also knew that I could help to raise awareness about sperm retrieval. If it wasn't for Laura knowing someone who'd lost their partner and wished they'd known about sperm retrieval, I wouldn't have had the choice either. I thought that if I could help one person to have a family in the same way I was, that would mean something.

So it was with nerves and excitement that I posted a photo of my bump on Instagram. I'd done an impromptu maternity shoot with a friend who was a photographer and the images she captured were beautiful. I certainly didn't feel like I had the pregnancy glow people talk about, but I loved my pregnant body and felt more confident than ever. I was still conscious that I didn't have a really noticeable bump. I have a long torso, so it took me a long time to really show. On the way to the grassy field where we did the shoot, we went through the McDonald's drive through and I stuffed my face with fries, nuggets and a thickshake to really fill my belly out. It did the trick.

I announced my pregnancy to the world with a photo of my tummy filled with Maccas, and the caption:

Bubba Chump coming this October.

Your Dad and I have been dreaming of you for years little one. With a heart-wrenching plot twist in the middle, I am honoured to finally welcome a piece of the phenomenon that is Chumpy back into the world!

When my love had his accident, we all held onto hope that I'd be pregnant that month. We'd been trying for a baby. IVF was on our cards, but it wasn't something I ever imagined I'd be tackling on my own.

Bittersweet like none other, I've never been more certain or excited about anything in my entire life.

Immediately, I was flooded with love and support from friends and strangers alike.

'I don't even know you, but sitting here with tears in my eyes for you and your families. What a joyful silver lining and how great is modern day science! Best of luck to you from one Mumma Bear to another,' someone wrote.

'I just cried. Oh my gosh!!! I've followed your story, Ellidy, and I've never seen or felt a soulmate story like yours and Chumpy. I am so happy for you. I lost my breath when I saw this. I hope he's a mini-Chump. With tears and love across the world,' another added.

'The universe has incredible ways to gift us what we've been hoping for. Many congratulations to you and to Chumpy watching over it all,' they continued.

Funnily enough, as soon as I posted the announcement, my morning sickness disappeared for my second trimester. It came back for the third one, but I didn't complain. My bump, hot chip craving and nausea made it all feel real. I was having a baby.

Most days, I hoped Chumpy was watching over it all. I was sure he'd have been happy that I was doing what we had always planned to do and having our baby, but he would have hated not being there for me. It would have hurt him so much, seeing me doing it all on my own. He would have wanted to be at every appointment, front row at all the prenatal classes and putting together all of the baby furniture. I can only imagine how particular – and pedantic – he would have been during my pregnancy. I'm sure I wouldn't have been eating quite as many hot chips if he was around! He would be making sure I was taking all my vitamins and eating enough vegetables.

On the days that his absence felt all-consuming, I reminded myself that I was carrying a piece of him within me.

CHAPTER THIRTEEN

A Year

They say time heals, but they never tell you how much time it takes.

Every 'first' was hard. The first time the baby kicked and Chumpy wasn't there to put his hand on my belly to feel it. The first time I went back to the Sea Bar Café in Dee Why, where Chumpy and I'd had coffee every morning when we lived in Sydney, I saw they'd named a breakfast dish after him. The Chumpy Haloumi Stack was his favourite meal. The first time I went down to Eden without Chumpy, Rummi ran through Chris and Sally's house looking for him. He wasn't there.

The first wedding I went to was in March 2021, nine months after Chump died. Like I said before, Chump was a champion at weddings. He loved them. I can still see him on the dance floor, with a massive grin and some dorky dance moves. I was a bridesmaid and Chump had teased the bride when she first asked me because we were trying for a baby. 'El's going to be basically giving birth or we will have a newborn by the time the wedding comes around, so are you sure you want her as your bridesmaid? She could be unreliable.'

Chump was right. When the wedding did come around, I was pregnant – with an embryo fertilised with the sperm we had retrieved from his body. It was like something out of a futuristic fever dream. He never would have been able to predict that. Who would?

We started to measure time by how long Chumpy had been gone. Days, then weeks, then months. There was WC (With Chumpy) and AC (After Chumpy). On the two-month anniversary of his passing, I went to Chumpy's Reef, as we call it now, and sat in the sand with my emotions. A perfect rainbow curled over the horizon as the sun set behind the waves.

On the eve of the six-month anniversary of his passing, I posted a photo on Instagram of us sitting on 'our rock' at Barrenjoey Headland one New Year's Day, with the caption:

Majestic Man

Tomorrow marks six months since Chumpy left our house one morning to go diving and never returned. I am still absolutely baffled. I replay our last moments together over and over in my head.

Lately I am needing and missing him more than ever. His absence is felt in every single encounter. I just cannot describe the heart-obliterating pain of losing your other half.

Coming up to the one-year mark, I didn't know how I was meant to feel. I did know that I didn't want to be alone for it; neither did Chump's parents, so they came up to stay with me.

Chris's birthday is on 4 July, so we spent the day together. We took Stella and Rummi to the beach and they ran and ran, herding imaginary sheep in the sand. For lunch, we went to a little café called Cubby in Chinderah, near where we held Chumpy's funeral at Melaleuca Gardens. It was sombre, but I think we all wanted to feel close to Chumpy however we could.

We took the long way home. Chris was driving his trusty LandCruiser with Sal riding shotgun, me in the back, the dogs in the tray covered in salt water and sand and Emma on loudspeaker, having a chat. We were driving on an old country backroad between Cabarita Beach and

Casuarina when Chris suddenly put his left indicator on and pulled over.

'What's going on?' we asked.

'Oh, I think I just saw a bit of plastic on the road back there. I'm going to go pick it up,' he said, unbuckling his seatbelt and opening the ute door. It was such a typical Pullin thing to do. They were always collecting rubbish from the beach, streets and bush.

Sal and I kept chatting to Em on the phone as we watched Chris in the rear-view mirror. He walked a hundred metres back and bent down in the middle of the road. When he came back to the car, he was holding a little tomahawk axe. Chumpy had sent his dad an axe for his birthday. Axes were so symbolic of Chumpy's relationship with his dad; they made one together, they had an uncanny affinity with the Vikings and Chumpy's first tattoo was of a giant axe on his ribs. What are the chances of Chris finding an axe in the middle of the road, out in the countryside, on his first birthday after losing Chump?

I didn't always believe in 'signs from above', but I do now. I have to. I can't fathom the idea that Chumpy is completely gone, that there are no traces left of him, that his energy has evaporated. I simply refuse to.

On the anniversary of Chumpy's death, my mum wrote

a farewell to him. It's still pinned to the noteboard in my pantry. She was the only one to call him Alex.

This is a tribute to and my thoughts on the passing of my son-in-law, Alex 'Chumpy' Pullin.

Thursday 8 July 2021 marked the first year of Chumpy's passing and as such life for my daughter, Ellidy, Alex's parents, Chris and Sally, his sister, Emma, has changed forever. His sudden and tragic death sent shockwaves through us all as well as extended family, friends and the worldwide community.

Exceptional is the word that readily comes to mind when I talk of Alex, a natural leader and decision maker who inspired all with his zest for life and his love and gratitude for all that he had in his life. With his inspirational and thought-provoking spirit, he ignited passion and truth in all who took notice.

His word was his bond and he planned everything with purpose, he meticulously and lovingly cared for all that he had in his life, most prominently my daughter, Ellidy, who was his centre.

I try not to look at photos of Alex lest I cry, but when I do look, the word majestic jumps out at me, for he truly was majestic with his stand-firm approach, his activism, passionate and strong ideals on environmental and social issues, and of course his love of sports and music. How I would have loved to watch him grow older and for those ideals to grow.

Our families are overwhelmed with great sorrow. My daughter awakens every day and chooses life – to live every day with hope and make a concerted effort to bring forth her infectious effervescence so that she can carry on Alex's legacy and make him proud of her and of their shared life that was. For every day she feels his presence and is comforted in the knowledge that he will never truly leave her. But in her private moments, she succumbs to immense sadness, which is almost too much for me, as her mother, to bear.

Alex … On the day of your death, I cradled your head in my hands and said a prayer over you – sorry about that by the way, I know you aren't religious – I thought to myself, if I could swap places with you, I would.

I often ponder why for some dynamic people life ceases to exist far too young. It's cruel and inexplicable that life can shift so swiftly and unexpectedly.

I now find I must stand tall, reset myself and steady the ship as both my children need my support. I am pivotal in helping navigate Ellidy through her grief, being her strength, as well as a safe and soft place to fall.

Also, for my son, David. He has suffered other losses and this last has affected him more than most realise. He

and Chumpy shared a deep bond and a kindred spirit –
with an albeit decidedly different delivery that marked their
individuality.

When great trees fall.

A very great tree has fallen and will leave an indelible
mark.

We weren't the only ones to mark the date.

The snowboarding community united on 8 July 2021 to
ShredForChumpy. Olympic athletes and novices alike hit
the slopes in Thredbo, Perisher, Hotham, Mount Buller
and Falls Creek in honour of Chumpy. It had been a
grizzly week in the mountains, but on that day, there was
sunshine on every single mountain from Victoria all the
way up to New South Wales.

'Someone was smiling down on us,' said Cam, who was
leading the pack at Thredbo. 'Being able to come together
and share our memories of Chumpy was really therapeutic.
That day was a big part of the healing process for a lot of
people – me included. It took me a long time to be able to
think about Chumpy without crying. Now I can remember
him and smile, but there are still tears.'

Mum was right, a great tree had fallen and left a huge
mark that stretched all the way from the beaches on the
Gold Coast to the mountains in the south. That was never

more obvious than on the anniversary of Chumpy's death. But it's obvious to me every day.

Being pregnant, dealing with my dad's diagnosis and working through the loss of Chump was a full-time job, but it didn't pay the bills. When Chumpy died, I vowed to do whatever I had to do to keep our home. Chumpy was the breadwinner in our family and then he was gone. I needed to step up to the plate to keep a roof over Rummi's head, but I didn't know where to start. It was hard to think about money and the mortgage when I was in the depths of despair, but it's something I had to do – like everyone who loses a loved one.

I'd studied a business degree, worked in an office job and then holiday rentals, and I did the odd modelling gig, but I'd never had a career per se. I always knew I would be a mum and so climbing the corporate ladder was never my goal. Chumpy was my life. I lived for him. Not in a weird devotee, unfeminist way, but in the sense that I wanted to support him in any way I could.

When my close friend Chloe came to me with a business idea to launch a podcast, I wasn't sure anyone would want to listen. The only podcasts I'd listened to were from medical experts about fertility and pregnancy, back when Chumpy and I were trying for a baby. I wasn't an expert in anything! Besides, Chumpy was the talker, not me. I hated public speaking. When our friends asked us both to MC their wedding, I went pale and Chump assured me he'd do all the talking. He knew my strengths and speaking wasn't one of them. Sure, I could be a chatterbox, but not in front of an audience.

'Who'd want to listen to us blabber on?' I asked.

'Uh, who wouldn't?' she replied, full of her trademark confidence. Chloe is such a go-getter and had already successfully launched her own businesses, including a swimwear line and a seltzer alcohol brand. But Chloe has her own heartbreaks. She and Fisher had been trying to have a baby for a few years and had dealt with the harsh reality of miscarriage too many times.

I like to say Chloe bullied me in to launching the *Darling, Shine!* podcast. At the start, she was certainly the driving force, but as we got rolling – and I realised how many people *did* want to listen to us blabber on – I was fully committed. So many people had reached out to ask about life as a widow, the sperm retrieval process and losing a loved one that I figured the podcast could be a good opportunity to answer all their questions in a candid and cathartic way.

We wanted *Darling, Shine!* to feel like a chat between friends. We didn't want it to just be about death and grief (my wheelhouse) or IVF and pregnancy loss (which Chloe sadly had experience in), but we did want to bring attention to the subjects that are hard to talk about and often swept under the rug. Our mission statement became to 'unpack the raw and often unspoken experiences of womanhood, grief, friendship and everything in between'.

Since we launched in 2021, we've interviewed other widows, including Lyndie Irons and Lotte Bowser; a Chinese medicine expert; a sexologist; a meditation guru; Chloe's IVF doctor, Doctor Kee Ong; mental health advocates and a vulva photographer. We've also shared our most personal stories and bared our souls for all to hear. I think that's what our listeners relate to most: our (sometimes brutal) honesty. We're flaws and all. Chloe has seen me at my worst and my best, as I have her. It's not easy talking about the hardest days of our lives, but it can be healing – for both us and our listeners.

After I lost Chump, I was surprised to feel grateful for social media, of all things. Through Instagram – and later *Darling, Shine!* – I was able to connect with so many widows around the world, and I've had hundreds of people share their stories of loss with me, lightening each other's loads. It made me feel less alone in my empty bed. If Chloe and I can make someone feel less alone on their hard days, that's pretty damn special.

I am proud of what we've created together as friends and business partners. *Darling, Shine!* has done incredibly well and it's how I earn my living. The success is something I struggle with constantly. I never would have started a podcast if Chumpy was still alive. I know that. I would've been a barefoot stay-at-home mum with a baby on my hip and hopefully another one on the way. Sometimes I worry that people will think I'm capitalising on my grief, but I never asked for any of this. And sharing my story has become an unexpected silver lining to a pretty fucked situation.

I'd trade it all in a second to have Chumpy back. But until a magic genie appears to grant my wish, I've got a mortgage to pay. And stories to share.

On what would have been Chumpy's thirty-fourth birthday – and the second one since his passing – I couldn't celebrate. I didn't have it in me. My friend had made a beautiful gluten-free cake – as was the tradition – but on the day, I told her I wasn't up to cutting it. The loss had started to sink in, and it all felt too real, too much, too hectic. I was struggling. We still ate the cake (it was sticky date pudding and I was heavily pregnant), but we didn't do all the birthday formalities.

In the years to come, I'd like to be able to celebrate Chumpy's birthday. Any excuse for cake, right? I imagine starting a tradition where I take Rummi and our baby down to Chumpy's Reef to mark the occasion. I don't want it to be a sad day, but grief doesn't care much about what you want. It just is.

CHAPTER FOURTEEN

A Fear

I wrote to my baby before she was born. In her baby book, I wrote:

> You are so lucky, you've got the best dad in the whole
> world. He's the biggest legend. I will show you everything
> he is – and was – but he's not here. And he won't be here.
> But you're so lucky that he's your dad.

When I was pregnant, Rummi would lick my belly. I tried to explain. 'There's a little piece of Chumpy in there. I know he's gone, it's shit and it sucks, but part of him is coming back – in here,' I'd say, dripping tears onto her fur. 'What would I do without you, Rummi? And you, Bubba Chump?'

I called the baby Bubba Chump, but I knew their actual last name would be Pullin. I wanted our kid to feel like they belonged to both of us, and to carry on Chumpy's legacy. For that to happen, I knew I had to change my name to Pullin as well. I was never not going to have the same last name as my baby.

When Chumpy was alive, we either would have eloped and had a small wedding ceremony, or changed my name before we had kids. Becoming a Pullin was inevitable. I just hadn't expected it to happen without Chump.

On a trip down to Sydney, I caught a bus and a train from the Northern Beaches to the NSW Registry of Births, Deaths and Marriages in the city to change my last name from Vlug to Pullin. Inside the grey corporate office, I filled out the paperwork. One of the questions on the form was, 'Why do you want to change your name?'

That's how I ended up writing the weirdest sentence I've ever written: 'My partner passed away a year ago and now I'm pregnant with his baby and I want to have the same name as the baby.'

I imagined the public servant reading my answer and thinking, 'What the heck?!' I was sure they would think I was lying. It was another surreal moment in a string of surreal moments. I felt like I had to keep hitting myself over the head with reality: wake up, this is real life.

I knew it was real when I kept getting messages from my mum on my way to the Births, Deaths and Marriages office and while I was there going through the rigmarole of red tape and paperwork.

Are you sure you don't want to add a nod to your Greek heritage while you're there?

Olympia would be a nice middle name.

What about Athena?

Or even a Greek word that you like the sound of.

You may as well, while you're at it.

Sitting in that soulless office, I really wasn't thinking about my Greek heritage. I was changing my name for one reason: because Chumpy had died and I was having our baby. It was a big deal to me and I took it quite seriously. Meanwhile Mum was going on about her ancestors in Greece. Classic Karen! I could always trust Mum to bring me back to reality and I love her for it.

It took a few weeks to be processed, but I was officially Ellidy Pullin. It should have been a moment of pure joy and excitement – becoming a family with the man I loved – but it was just a bundle of forms in a tired city office.

After my baby news broke, my manager sent me an email asking if I had time to do an interview and photoshoot with *Vogue Australia* the following week. Um, I would *make* time. IT WAS FUCKING *VOGUE*!

All my friends had the same – expletive filled – reaction as me. We just about fell off our chairs at the thought of me being in the holy grail of fashion magazines.

The sky over the Gold Coast turned it on for the shoot. The water reflected the moody clouds and made for a hell of a dramatic background. You couldn't have painted or photoshopped a more beautiful scene. We did the shoot just down the road from my house, at Chumpy's Reef. I walked back and forth along the stretch of sand where Chump and I had taken Rummi to run countless times. Rummi came to the shoot, of course. And stole the show, naturally. The photographer would try to capture a solemn moment of me and my bump only to have Rummi run past and photobomb with a random tail or a flick of sand.

As *Vogue* shoots go, mine was pretty low-key. I had my hair and make-up done at my house and dressed myself. The photographer, Jamie Green, had a small team and the energy was light. I wanted to enjoy the day and be present in the moment. I tried not to think too hard about the reasons why I was standing on the beach posing for a *Vogue* photographer – I didn't want my mascara

This axe on Chumpy's ribs is a symbol of battle, hard work and perseverance. Chump designed his axe tattoo with the words 'ALL IN' in Viking runes down the handle of the axe. This was Chumpy's first tattoo and on the day I was telling him to get it smaller because he has such perfect skin and a body free of ink. I was worried it would be too much. But he was adamant it was going to take up most of his ribs! It took me a few days but I fell in love with it, and that made him so happy! Chump and his dad then carved and restored an actual wooden axe that his dad found in the bush near their house. He then got another tattoo of a mystical skeleton man and the words 'SEE YOU OUT THERE'.

I definitely feel like this one speaks to me.

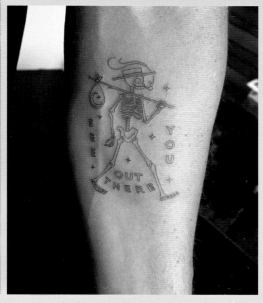

Me and Bro at the paddle out for Chumpy at Palm Beach, on the Gold Coast. This took place just three days after Chump left this earth. Safe to say our heads were in a complete fog! Bro and I stayed out in the water for a while after everyone paddled in. A perfect left-hander came my way and I caught it in to shore where all my girlfriends from Sydney were there to cuddle me.

Me, Dadlet and Bro.

This was the cutest day ever (left). Chump took this photo. It was the last time he and Dad saw each other, not long before Chump passed away. As borders were closing because of Covid, Dad rode all the way up to Queensland from New South Wales on his motorbike (took him nine hours) to give us a cuddle at the border and then turned around. Dad would have had cancer at this point but we had no idea, he seemed healthy and happy as!

All my friends told me they thought I was having a boy – a mini Alex – but I knew from the moment I lay down on the IVF clinic table that I was having a little girl. I didn't find out before the birth because I wanted it to be a surprise. Regardless of whether the baby was a boy or a girl, they were a fucking miracle. And she is – being a mum to Minnie Alex Pullin is the best thing I have ever done.

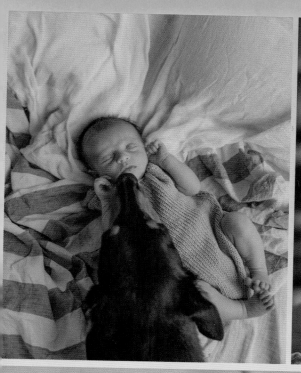

Me and Minnie (below);
Minnie with Mum and Bro
(right); with Dad (bottom).

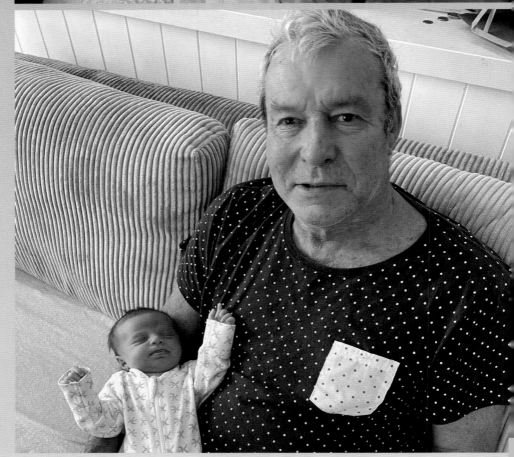

Minnie with Chris and
Sally (left); Rummi
with little sis (below).

Now I am a mum I have even more respect for mine. I don't think I properly appreciated how strong she is and how hard it must have been for her with two kids and no money. The way she looked after Chumpy that awful day and the way she looks after me and Minnie now is epic.

Rummi, me and Minnie – our little family. 'If not with you, then for you.'

to run – but at the same time, I was fully aware that I was there to share the story of Chumpy and me and our unborn baby. I wasn't a celebrity or a high-end model who would typically be found in the pages of *Vogue*. I was an expectant mum – against all odds – who had something to say.

In the interview with the *Vogue* journalist Remy Rippon, I was determined to show that hope trumps pain. 'I feel lucky that Chumpy was who he was; in life and in loss, Chumpy is the gift that keeps giving,' I said. 'In many ways, it simply feels like I'm carrying the torch of our future. It sits differently to how it did before, but there's still something familiar; I still use Chumpy's toothbrush (it's electric!), I still sing out "Hey, Chumpy" whenever I pass his music studio in our home, and some day very soon, a little piece of Chumpy will be back in my arms again.'

At the shoot, I cupped that little piece of Chumpy in my belly with my hands as I waded through the shallow water. It was a precious moment to have – and even more so to be captured on film.

When the September 2021 issue of *Vogue* hit stands, I rushed down to the newsagency with Lizzo, sat on the floor and flipped through the pages until I found my story. It was unbelievable. I grabbed my face in disbelief and ran my fingers over the pages to make sure it was real. Then I cried.

I knew Chumpy would've been proud of me. He wouldn't have had a clue what *Vogue* magazine was, but he would've loved seeing me all hyped up and giddy about it. Sitting on the floor of my local newsagency, I was like a little kid in a lolly shop on their birthday. Chumpy would have joked about me acting like a child, but he would've also got a kick out of it.

People have asked me what it's like to grieve publicly. It's a hard question to answer because I don't know any different. Chumpy was a well-known and loved sportsman, so people were always going to be interested in and feel connected to his death. Even if I didn't start the podcast, share openly on Instagram or give magazine interviews, people would still be curious and have questions – especially after they found out I was pregnant with Chumpy's baby. I don't blame them, it's a weird story!

I genuinely think being able to grieve openly has been a blessing. Talking publicly about my loss has been a much-needed outlet to work through my emotions (and a cheap form of therapy). Not many people get asked about their grief more than the standard, 'How are you coping?' Because I get so many messages and speak about what I'm going through on *Darling, Shine!*, I can really go deep.

I know not everyone can vocalise their grief like me, and I'm grateful for the outlets I have. Even when the words are hard to say or the thoughts hurt to remember, it always feels healthy to do. I'm better for it. And I like to think others are better for it as well.

I've never told anyone this. It's taken me six months to admit it to myself. I was consumed with fear for the entire third trimester of my pregnancy. My standard setting is to be happy-go-lucky, but really, I was a wreck of nerves. The only person I shared that with was Mum. I was terrified something would go wrong. I didn't want to admit it to anyone because that would mean saying it out loud, which was very unlike me. I usually share my feelings freely.

I know it's normal for expectant mothers to be nervous. But what I felt was so much more than that, it was genuine fear and an unshakeable feeling that I was going to lose my baby, just like I'd lost the first IVF transfer, and just like I'd lost Chumpy.

In the countdown to my due date, the doctors had told me my baby was small and they asked me to come in for scans every week to monitor the baby's growth. On the outside, I was easy, breezy El. On the inside, I was terrified.

I was sure something was wrong with the baby. I kept running the numbers in my mind. We collected Chumpy's sperm in the thirty-seventh hour. Only one per cent of it was alive. The baby was below the tenth percentile.

At each scan, they'd take a 3D sonogram photo of the baby and in every single image, the baby was looking in the opposite direction. I desperately wanted to see their face – or anything that mildly resembled a baby – but all I got were blurs of grey. Out of sixteen-odd ultrasound photos, not a single one showed the baby's face.

I told myself that the baby was just busy talking to Chump. He was teaching them everything they had to know before they were born. I joked that they were camera-shy, unlike their mum. But inside my head, another voice spoke over the hopeful and joking thoughts. The voice cut straight to my core, telling me that there was something wrong with my baby. Why did I have to have so many scans? It whispered all my worst fears.

I kept these fears tight to my chest. My worries were my own and I carried them around with me every day. I thought if I shared them out loud that I would breathe truth into them. As much as I loved being pregnant, my fears hid in the corners of my joy.

Don't get me wrong, there was still a lot of joy. I went on a babymoon to Brisbane with Lizzo just before she was due to pop. We'd booked a room at The Calile Hotel on James Street, and as we pulled into the carpark, the numberplate on the car in front of us was 'ELMO92.' It was Chumpy's nickname for me, and the year I was born. It brought back a memory I'd almost forgotten ...

A year earlier, we'd been on our way to the very same hotel in Brisbane for Lizzo's birthday with Chloe. It was two months after Chumpy had passed away, and the plan was to drink ourselves silly beside the pool. On our way there, we were driving up the highway and passed a guy on a motorbike who was wearing a bright red fluffy Elmo costume. We screamed out the window at him and he waved back at us, and we drove the whole way to Brissy in an odd convoy. It was such a sign.

Chumpy always found a way to be there with me.

Back home on the Gold Coast, my baby shower was such a beautiful day. My friends organised everything and I just sat back and enjoyed myself. They must have raided every supermarket and fresh fruit stall in the area because there were bowls of lemons, limes and oranges everywhere, as well as olive branches. They turned my Gold Coast house into a European oasis. Mum was right at home in our faux Greece.

The highlight of the day was the drinking competition. Trust my friends to organise a drinking game for a baby shower! I couldn't participate, but I watched on as my mates raced to scull their mimosas from the teats of baby bottles.

Each of my friends gave me a bead with a note explaining the energy they wanted to impart to me ahead of the birth. I strung the beads together and carried their gifts – strength, courage, presence – with me.

At the end of the shower, we took a group photo on my deck by the pool. I'd had the deck finished with a concrete render daybed area after Chumpy died, just as we'd always planned on doing. Stamped in the concrete were the words 'Chumpy's deck'. In the photo, I'm beaming, but behind my smile, the fear was ever present. I was so ready to have my baby, not least because I was excited to meet them, but also because I knew the fear would only lift once I was holding them in my arms and knew they were real and healthy and nothing was wrong.

Along with the pack of tiny white Bonds singlets Chumpy and I had bought, I started to fill up the nursery with gifts from the baby shower and all the necessities. My amazing friend Maia had a portrait done of Chumpy and I hung it above the crib. My mum – who is still the most fashionable woman I know and creates magic with her sewing machine – turned two of Chumpy's t-shirts into little baby rompers.

The nursery was set, the hospital bag was packed and I was ready to go. On 19 October 2021, I posted a photo of a young Chumpy on Instagram and a caption:

I can't wait to look into our bub's eyes and see you again, Chump! We will be forever frolicking right by the sea, where we know you will be.

PART THREE

What Became

'Look up and get lost

I'm not in a fog

I'm here'

— Alex 'Chumpy' Pullin, unpublished lyrics, 2016

CHAPTER FIFTEEN

Bubba Chump

I felt like a lion in a cage; roaring, fierce, ready to fight. I was in active labour for eight hours and every time a contraction seized my body, I felt like a wild animal. I told my midwife after the fact and she said I actually seemed quite calm on the outside.

I had pretty clear expectations of what I wanted for my birth. My mum had both me and my brother after two hours of active labour, so I thought I'd go into the hospital and pop the baby out. I pictured myself having a waterbirth in the hospital's birthing suite, and knew I wanted it to be as low-intervention as possible.

Of course, absolutely nothing went to plan. When I first stepped into the bath at the hospital, it became immediately apparent it was designed for someone half my height. My legs didn't fit at all and trying to squeeze into it, I looked like a gangly – very heavily pregnant – giraffe.

In the week leading up to the birth, I had three 'stretch and sweeps' to encourage labour. My midwife put her hand up my vagina and reached for my cervix to create movement between the membrane around the baby's head and the vaginal opening. It's a pretty standard procedure, but because my cervix was so far back, it felt like she was digging to China.

I was two centimetres dilated for the entire week before I gave birth. So every night for a week, I went to bed thinking I'd wake up in labour. 'It's happening tonight, it's happening tonight,' I'd tell myself.

Every day, I walked up and down the Currumbin stairs, I bounced on my exercise ball and went to my acupuncturist. I thought I'd give birth at any moment. Every time I felt a twinge, I thought it was go-time. But the week rolled on and on.

Most days, I called my neighbour Max to bring me supplies. Every time, he'd answer the phone saying, 'Do you need me to take you to the hospital?'

And every time, I'd say, 'Not yet. But have you got any chocolate you can chuck over the fence for me?'

Everyone was on high alert. My mum was on standby and all of my friends were constantly at me for updates. Rummi was especially clingy.

After a week of anticipation, I wrote in my journal.

Sunday 24 October, 2021

Woke up feeling a bit fucked. Cramping from 4:30 am. Sensations of having to do a number two. Swaying back and forth on the ball, I felt like Chump was right beside me, holding me.

Mum just started asking about my birth plan and what she wants to do when we rock up to the hospital. THAT'D BE RIGHT KAREN. Not really living up to your name, are you, mate?

The cramps aren't painful, probably about forty-five seconds long and five or six minutes apart.

Mum's lucky I didn't have a detailed birth plan and hand her orders. I always got confused when people thought they could 'plan' a vaginal birth and wrote notes and instructions. Birthing (and life) rarely go to schedule and so I was one hundred per cent going with the flow. My only certainty about the whole thing was that if I died during birth, I wanted Chloe and Fisher to raise my baby, seeing as they wanted one so badly and I knew they would make the best parents in the world.

I spent the day at home relaxing with my mum, brother and our friends. We were sitting around, laughing and having a chat. I felt relaxed and ready. I had nothing to compare the pain to. I breathed through every contraction and genuinely felt excited when I had one. When two strangers – a mother and her daughter, who follow me on Instagram – knocked on my door, I gave the daughter a hug. It was pretty bad timing, but I didn't really mind.

I explained I was actually in labour, saying, 'Yeah, I've got a bit on.'

Everything was chill. Until it wasn't.

At about 4 pm – after twelve hours of early labour at home – Mum drove me to the hospital. It was only when I got in the car that I started to feel nauseous and unwell.

I always joke with Mum about how we'd had all day for her to put on a practical outfit, but she insisted on wearing a tight mini dress with a belt around the waist and clog heels. I kid you not. Mum simply cannot dress down. It was a classic Karen moment; she was always going to be the best-dressed grandma in the hospital.

I had imagined myself being pushed through the hospital in a wheelchair, but when we got there, I walked into the birthing suite on my own. In between my contractions,

I felt fine. But when the contractions came, they *came*. I ran into my midwife in the hallway and as soon as I saw her, I vomited on cue. Luckily, she had a spew bag on her. Ever the professional.

In the hospital room, I had the string of beads from my friends hanging up near a picture of Chumpy and Rummi. I'd also brought crystals, lavender oil and fairy lights with me to set the scene. As soon as we got into the suite and I'd set everything up, everything slowed down.

I alternated between the tiny bath and shower, searching for relief. The feeling of the water on my back was euphoric. The only time Mum took her heels off was when she had to get in the shower with me to get me through a particularly tough contraction.

Mum video-called Chloe in America for me when I was in the shower, and I was champing at the bit to have the baby. Meanwhile, Chloe was drunk. She'd just got home from a night out. She only vaguely remembers the phone call.

I'd been in active labour for two hours when I started to get restless. 'When is this baby coming? I thought they'd be here by now. Mum said it'd just pop out in an hour or two. What's going on?'

I could tell from my mum's body language that she was worried. She was tense and kept having to leave the room. I assumed she was just struggling seeing her daughter in pain, and I was so in the moment that I wasn't excessively concerned. I simply didn't have the capacity to be. I had given myself over to the process.

Even though I wanted a low-intervention birth, I had to have my waters broken. It wasn't quite as dramatic as I'd seen in films – a tsunami didn't gush out from between my legs – but it certainly got things moving.

No matter how many pregnancy podcasts you listen to or books you read or conversations you have, nothing can prepare you for the pain of labour. People tell you it hurts and I expected that. But I didn't understand just how much it would huuurrrttt. At some point in my pregnancy, someone had told me to visualise myself walking over the Sydney Harbour Bridge when I was in labour to take my mind off the pain. And I did. I kept imagining me and Chump walking back and forth across the harbour, hand in hand. We would've done some serious kilometres in my mind. I don't know how much it helped. Towards the end, every time a contraction hit, I thought I was going to die. I remember looking my mum in the eye and silently asking her if this was it – if I was dying – and pleading for her to save me.

The baby must have taken after me, because they were positioned on the right side of my body and corkscrewed towards the back of my spine instead of straight down and out. They clearly weren't the sharpest tool in the shed, I joked to the midwife in between contractions. The pain on my spine was excruciating. There was no way I was meditating my way out of the agony. Everything hurt and I was freezing cold, even though everyone else in the room was sweating. I had this weird fever come over me mid labour. It was a cold snap.

The midwives kept checking the baby's heartrate and that worried me as well. If the baby's heartrate was too high or too low, we would have had to get them out straightaway.

Knowing the baby's heartrate was fine gave me some comfort. Even if I was in a world of pain, they were doing good. If the baby was stressed, I would have been a wreck.

I so wanted to feel Chumpy's presence through the birth. I remember asking out loud if he was there. 'Excuse me, Chump, are you even here helping me from above? Because it doesn't feel like it, mate. It's really fucking painful.'

I started pushing. And kept pushing for four hours. It was hard work. I was on all fours when I looked up to see my student midwife sitting in front of me. 'Oh hi, how are you?' I greeted her. She'd actually been in the room for several hours, but I was so out of it I hadn't noticed.

When the baby's head crowned, my midwives and Mum started cheering me on. 'Come on, El, you've got this. One more contraction, you can do it. Just one more.'

They must have said 'one more' about a hundred times. It went on and on. Push after push. Guttural screams between untameable moans. My throat was raw from yelling out. I'm sure I nearly ripped my student midwife's arms off; I was holding on for dear life.

I don't know how I didn't pass out from exhaustion. I'd never been more physically tired. When the baby's head finally started to poke through, my midwife told me when to stop and start pushing, to try to avoid tearing. Every muscle in my body wanted to push, but I had to keep stopping so I didn't split in half. It was such a weird feeling.

'They've got hair,' the midwife said when the head popped out. I gave one last push and the rest of the baby slipped out. It was this extraordinary feeling of relief and pride and overwhelming love. In a moment, my baby was in my arms, a little girl. I knew it.

I looked into her eyes and I saw her dad. I saw Chumpy.

My mum cut the umbilical cord and I could see she was filled with the same emotions as me: relief, pride and overwhelming love. Mum was truly amazing through the whole thing. I couldn't have done it without her.

The baby was born with quite an olive complexion, and the first thing Mum said was, 'Look, she's Greek!' I half-expected Mum to pull out a bottle of olive oil to rub it into her skin in a sort of Greek christening.

We were both crying so hard. I had to keep wiping the tears away so I could look at my perfect, sweet baby. During the labour, I fully understood why people only had one kid. But as soon as I saw her, I felt like I could do it all over again. It took me hours to catch my breath. It was like I'd run a marathon – and won.

Minnie Alex Pullin was born on Monday 25 October 2021 at 2.50 am. As she took her first mouthfuls of air, I held her to my chest next to the necklace I wear that's imprinted with Chumpy's fingerprint. My two loves, close to my heart. Chumpy had been gone for fifteen months, but there I was, holding our daughter.

They say meeting your baby for the first time is a euphoric moment. And it was, but my lasting memory of giving birth to Minnie was of how she slipped out of me like a slippery little slug. When she was passed to me, all I could think about was how slippery she was and how I didn't want to drop her. I was relieved to hear her cry, and to see that she had two legs, but the rest is a blur.

After the doctors stitched me up, I was taken from the birthing suite back to my hospital room, where I watched Minnie sleep. I was mesmerised by the rise and fall of her chest. I kept thinking I'd fallen asleep and that I was dreaming. 'Is there really a baby in that bassinet next to me? Is it my baby? Is she finally here?' I thought. When the reality sunk in, the fear I'd carried with me through my third trimester lifted.

If Minnie was a miracle, my midwives were my guardian angels. After my midwife had safely delivered my baby, filled out all the hospital paperwork for me and cleaned me up, she went and made me two toasted cheese sandwiches with extra butter. I hadn't eaten for a full day, so it was the best thing ever, aside from Minnie.

My midwife later told me that she was working with another expectant mum at the same time as me. That woman's partner was one of the lifeguards on the beach who'd tried to save Chumpy. We gave birth within days of each other. My midwife told me the couple often thought of me and Chumpy.

There's a strange mix of sadness and strength knowing that I did it on my own. But I also know I wasn't really alone – Chumpy was with me the whole way.

The more time passes, the more the pain of the birth fades in my memory. In reality, eight hours of active labour isn't that long. A lot of women spend a day or more in that position. Even though I didn't have the waterbirth I imagined – and I didn't pop Minnie out in two hours, like my mum did with me – the birth did go according to plan. I had Minnie without drugs, I had only minimal tearing, and I had a beautiful, healthy baby girl. I would do it all over again a hundred more times ... but I might have the epidural next time.

CHAPTER SIXTEEN

Noonie

Babies cry. That's what my midwife told me when I left the hospital with my newborn daughter, and that's what I reminded myself every afternoon at witching hour. I approached new motherhood in the same way I went through life: without sweating the small stuff. I was never going to wrap my baby in cottonwool or hover over them like a helicopter parent. I didn't read all the parenting books or google the different reasons baby cry, I just listened to my intuition and went with that.

I know Chumpy would've been the exact opposite, but I couldn't second-guess, I had to learn to trust myself. In a lot of ways, that's how Chumpy was raised by Chris and Sal. They didn't follow the 'rules' – they took Chump on his first sailing trip when he was three months old – and they did what they felt was right for them and their kids. They winged it, and look at how good Chumpy and Emma turned out!

Apart from the obvious sleepless nights, dirty nappies and leaking boobs, I didn't see my life changing dramatically. I still got up every morning to walk Rummi at the beach, just with Minnie strapped to my chest in her baby carrier. I still had friends over for drinks, though I stuck to one glass of wine or a margarita. And I still kept working and recording the podcast, though I took a few months' 'maternity leave' from the admin side of things. Having a baby only changed my life for the better.

For the most part, Minnie was an angel newborn. She slept and she shat and she cried. Thankfully, she didn't need perfect silence to sleep, because that was never going to happen in my household. Both me and my friends can be very loud, so she must have gotten used to the volume when she was in my tummy. On the outside, she could sleep at noisy cafés in the stroller, in the car with the radio playing and on a towel in the shade at the beach with the sound of the waves crashing on the shore. As well as her ability to sleep anywhere, Minnie also inherited my spectacular spewing skills and mastered the art of projectile vomiting all over herself and me. I love that for us.

We brought Minnie home two days after she was born. Minnie was wrapped up in her striped hospital blanket and Rummi wore a bandana around her neck with her official new title: *Big Sister.* When Minnie was sleeping on my lap, Rummi would lie with her head resting on Minnie's tummy. My little family.

Just like her dad and Rummi, aka Rum-Dog Millionaire and Rumbledore, Minnie was given her fair share of nicknames: Min-Dog, Minichiello and Noonie.

We took Minnie for her first dip in the ocean when she was just a few weeks old. She hated it! But I'm sure she has her dad's salt water running through her veins and will grow up to love the sea as much as he did, and as much as I do.

As she gets older, I see more and more of Chumpy in Minnie. She's so present and aware. Sometimes I'll see her staring intensely into space, and I'll think, 'What are you looking at? Is your dad there?'

I still catch myself going to call out to Chumpy when Minnie's doing something cute. I still have entire conversations with him in my mind. He's still the first person I want to tell when something good or bad happens. Does that feeling ever go away? I hope not.

Even though he's not here, Chumpy is still so much a part of Minnie's life. I play his music when I'm feeding her, and in the car, and when she's having a bath. I take her down to Chumpy's Reef and we watch the sunset together. I tell her every day how much her dad loves her.

I want to bring Minnie up on love and happiness, not grief and sadness. I had Chump and lost him but, in essence, she hasn't lost him. I don't want people looking at her and feeling sad that her amazing Dad isn't with her physically. I want people to look at her and smile that she's been made possible. I am going to give Minnie a good life, that's what her Dad and I always wanted for our children. And Chump is always going to be a part of her and a presence in Minnie's life. She will know how he loves her because I know he does.

It's true what they say, having a baby gives you a new lease on life. I've started to see the world through Minnie's eyes: the feeling of sand between your toes at the beach, the different shades of green in the leaves on the trees and the sounds of the birds at sunrise. Minnie has given me a new perspective on the fragility of life. She is proof that anything is possible and we can't take a second for granted. I'm going to give this kid the best life I possibly can.

When Minnie was a month old, Chloe and her sisters babysat while I had a five-hour nap at her house. They brought Minnie in to be fed then took her back out to burp and change her while I went back to sleep. In that moment, I felt what it would have been like to be parenting with a partner. It was amazing. I have the best friends in the world.

I've had women who are contemplating becoming a single parent message me to ask for advice. I can only speak from my experiences, but the rewards of having Minnie have far outweighed the challenges we've faced together. Having Minnie is the best thing I'll ever do. You can never go wrong with creating life. And babies are the best things in the world.

I try not to put pressure on myself to be both Minnie's mum and dad. She's lucky to have two father figures in her life – in my brother, Dave, and our friend Fisher – so I don't feel the need to fill that void. There's no point worrying about what I can't give Minnie, so instead I focus on what I can give her: lots of love, fun adventures and a boob in her mouth when she's hungry.

I was worried about breastfeeding because it was something I really wanted to get right. I knew it didn't come easily to a lot of mothers, so I was conscious it might not be something we'd be able to do. Straight after I gave birth to Minnie, I worked hard to make sure we nailed our latching and feeding techniques. Once we did that, I started pumping as much as I could so I had plenty of milk supply. I always had a stack of milk stored in the freezer because I got into the habit of pumping consistently. I was lucky that Minnie loved to suck on anything – a boob, a bottle, her dummy, my nose – so she took to breastfeeding like a pro.

I don't buy into the made-up term 'mum guilt'. Women are constantly made to feel guilty for the things we do and don't do – if we work, if we don't, if we have a nanny, if we don't, if we leave our kids with their grandparents for a couple of hours to have a margarita, if we accidentally have too many margaritas and need to use pumped milk or formula for the bedtime feed – it's bullshit. Mothers don't have enough hands to juggle raising kids *and* carry around guilt.

For my first Mother's Day, my friend and jeweller Natalie Marie asked me to write some words on the significance of my ring – the one Chumpy and I designed together using my grandmother's diamonds and sapphires – the one she made for me after he died.

'How does your Natalie Marie jewellery piece mark your journey to motherhood?' she asked. I answered:

When I look down at my ring, I remember the face of my little girl's father who designed it with me before he passed. It's not a fine, dainty or delicate ring. It's sturdy with blue sapphires and diamonds, set deep into the thick gold band.

The ring is strong and resilient. When I look at the stones, I feel my little girl's daddy nurturing us from above. I feel him reminding me that I'm brave and strong. I feel him guiding me to be a fearless mother and trust my instincts. The ring reminds me that I can take on anything. I know my little girl will wear this ring with the same pride one day too.

CHAPTER SEVENTEEN

Her Father's Eyes – by Chris Pullin

Minnie had Chumpy's eyes when she was born. I saw so much of my son in Minnie when Sally and I first met her when she was six weeks old. She'd inherited his high cheekbones, his chunky baby leg rolls and his absolute awe for the world that surrounds us. I think if I drew a little moustache on Minnie, she'd be the spitting image of her dad.

Sal and I were quite involved with Ellidy's IVF process. We felt her heartache when the first embryo didn't take and shared her joy when the second one was a goer. We weren't really thinking about ourselves in those moments – we didn't imagine being grandparents or rocking our grandchild to sleep or teaching them how to play the ukulele. We were purely thinking about Ellidy and hoping for the best. For her.

We have the utmost love and respect for El – that can't be torn apart. There's a sense of ease between us that can only be felt between family members.

It's hard not to imagine what could have been. You only need to look at how Chumpy was with Rummi to know what he would have been like as a father. From the minute Chumpy got Rummi, she wasn't just a dog, she was a Pullin; part of the family. He gave her so much time and love – and he would have given his child that as well.

Chump would have been Minnie's greatest advocate, her greatest friend and her greatest teacher. She would have been so proud of him – he would have made sure of that. I like to think Chumpy would have raised his kids with the same adventurous spirit we brought him up with, as well as the deep sense of family that we cherish. I imagine Minnie would rush home from school every day, excited to see her mum and dad, and to see what unorthodox experience they had planned for her that afternoon.

We met Minnie at the hospital; not the hospital she was born in, but the hospital where Sal was being treated for cancer. Sal had been diagnosed with lymphoma of the brain in September 2021, a full year after we lost our son and the same month he would've turned thirty-four.

El took a photo of Sal holding Minnie for the first time and you can see the love in her eyes. I want to take Minnie camping, to teach her how to sail on the boat, to watch her catch her first fish and to help her make something out of wood in my shed. When Chumpy was at home in Eden, he was always making shit in the shed, little wooden boxes and axe handles. I want to give my granddaughter all the love her dad had growing up – and all the love he'd have given her if he was still here.

Sometimes, people who've seen our story on the news tell us how wonderful it must be for us to be grandparents now. When I see a photo of Minnie, my first thought is always, 'Where the fuck is Chumpy? He should be here.' It hurts us to live without Chumpy, but what hurts more is knowing what he's missing out on.

When Sally got sick, Chumpy would have been the first person sitting beside her hospital bed, holding her hand and telling her it was all going to be okay. After her diagnosis, Sal spent six months in hospital, undergoing treatment. It was six months of scans, appointments, hospital food, pain and devastating sickness. To see Sal literally shrinking – disappearing – was torture. Cancer isn't something you'd wish on your worst enemy.

It took its toll. We needed our son and he wasn't there. Cancer is a battle and Sal is fighting, and we're all cheering her on. But Chumpy would have been her biggest cheerleader.

Sally was always the soft place to land in our family. She was the one who taught Chumpy how to cook when he went overseas on his own the first time. She was the one who put the kids to bed nicely and who passed down her musical talents. If the kids needed a hug, help with their homework or a moment of gentleness, Sal was there. The bond between Sal and Chump was something else. It's hard to express just how close they were. There's so much of her in him. Even in the busiest room, Chump always managed to seek Sally out.

Sal took care of Chump all his life, and I know he would have wanted to take care of her.

In a way, it feels like we've been cheated out of mourning our boy because we've been busy fighting for Sal's life. It's been one blow after another. Some days, I just want to throw my hands in the air and say, 'Fuck it!' But I've got Sally to look after, and Emma, and Ellidy and Minnie. I feel very responsible for them all. Besides, I couldn't do anything that would disappoint Chumpy. I'm not the most spiritual bloke, but if he's up there, looking down on me and judging my actions, I want him to be proud of me.

Sally has finished treatment and is home now with me and Stella. This morning, we took a walk on the beach together, which might sound pretty insignificant, but considering she had to basically learn how to walk again after her treatment and being bed-ridden for six months, it was a small triumph.

We don't know what the future looks like. It's my hope that we can get back to living a life that has some satisfaction, even if that's just feeling the sun on our faces on a walk at the beach.

Chumpy was at home on the water. The sea isn't the same without him. When Chump was about two years old, we bought a boat from South Australia called *Morning After* and sailed it back to the east coast. He was only a little fella, but he knew that the water was supposed to be on the outside of the boat – not the inside – so when the toilet starting overflowing with seawater, he shouted out, 'Emergency, water!' These are the memories that keep me warm. They're also the memories that break my heart.

There's not a moment that goes by that I don't think about Chumpy and, in turn, Ellidy and Minnie. It's my hope that El will one day find a person and be able to love again. It will be a different kind of love, of course, but she deserves to live a happy and normal life. She's too young to be single forever. We'd like to see her go on to create some sort of relationship when she's ready.

After Chumpy's funeral, Emma and her band Los Pintar wrote a song for him called 'Sweet King'. It's a beautiful tribute to her brother and her best friend, but it hurts me too much to listen to it. I can hear the pain in Em's voice when she sings the second verse:

I never thought of you
As someone who could disappear
Now every thought's of you
Why stick around if you ain't here
I made it long for you
The pieces near me are healing I guess
I'll leave them here for you
Shine down some light while I deal with this mess
Sleep now my king

I keep the axe I made with Chumpy on the wall of our staircase. Every morning when I get up and go downstairs, I touch it and I think of Chump. Sometimes I say the words of his forearm tattoo, 'See you out there'. Sometimes I don't say anything at all.

CHAPTER EIGHTEEN

The Last Laugh

Minnie was three weeks old when I got the call: my dad wasn't doing too good. He was getting increasingly unsteady on his feet, spending most of the day in bed and becoming more confused and emotional. When Dad was diagnosed with the tumour in August 2020, the doctors gave him four months to live. He'd lasted fourteen months. He'd been hanging on for us, but I didn't know how much longer he could keep his grasp.

So, two-and-a-half weeks after giving birth, with leaking boobs and a baby bag full of nappies and postpartum pads, I packed Minnie into the car. I flew one of my friends up to the Gold Coast from Sydney so she could road trip down with us. I don't think I could have physically – or mentally – done the trip with Minnie on my own. My friend did most of the driving, Minnie did a lot of sleeping. On the way, we stopped at Crescent Head, where my brother and I used to go camping at the beach with Dad. We had so many happy, sun-drenched, sea-kissed memories at Cresent; catching perfect waves, drinking raspberry lemonade at the pub and surviving on fish and chips.

I tried to make the best out of the trip I desperately wished I didn't need to make. I should have been at home in a bubble of new motherhood, recovering and bonding with my daughter. Instead, I was sitting in the passenger seat on the Pacific Highway, pumping breastmilk and trying to keep it all together.

When we arrived in Sydney, my dad looked like an older version of himself. He was pretty out of it. He could still take a few steps, but was mostly using a wheelchair to get around. I called my brother. 'It's touch and go. You'd better get down here.'

When Bro arrived a couple of days later, Dad could no longer walk at all. He was incontinent and unable to feed, wash or dress himself. He'd lost the use of the left side of his face and body, so when he'd have a drink, it would dribble out of the corner of his mouth. We knew it was only a matter of time. He was going downhill, and it was hard to watch, but it would have been harder to not be there with him.

I remember seeing Dad in the wheelchair and thinking, *I'll never see my dad walk again. He'll never give me another proper hug. He won't come back from this.* I had a little cry, but I didn't dwell on it in front of Dad. He was too busy cracking jokes to be upset.

Introducing Dad to Minnie was the most surreal moment. I don't think he could believe his baby had had a baby. He kept staring at her and saying, 'She's so tiny. I thought she'd be bigger.'

'Yeah, that's because she's fresh out of the womb, Dad,' I'd reply.

Minnie and Dad spent days sleeping side by side. It was the most adorable sight. I know within my heart that Dad had been holding on because he wanted to meet Minnie. Then when he met her, he kept holding on because he wanted to hang out with her and me and my brother, just a little longer.

In between the days he didn't get out of bed, Dad had random bursts of energy. Sometimes it felt like he'd get a second wind, that maybe he'd last another year. In those moments, Bro and I took Dad on adventures, like he took us when we were little. We'd get him into the wheelchair with a sarong covering his lap in typical Holiday Pete fashion, and take him for an excursion – you'd better believe we took that wheelchair off road.

Dad was happiest when he was on the road, at the Terrey Hills Tavern or in nature. We couldn't bear seeing him just laying there inside.

Not long before he was diagnosed, Dad bought himself a brand-new motorbike, a Suzuki V-Strom. Dad never bought anything brand new so this was special! It was a beauty and we hate that he didn't get to ride it more but his body and mind started to let him down. Dad and Bro (and Chump) loved their motorbikes. One day, Dad said to Bro, 'Let's go for a ride.' They left from Dad's place at Warriewood and rode out to Palm Beach. They loved riding around the Bilgola bends. Often, before, Dad and Chump would do this same ride together, and sometimes I'd go on the back of Chump's bike and then swap half way and ride back with Dad.

This time, when Dad and Bro got to Palmy, Dad said, 'You wanna swap and ride this one back, Dave?' He didn't have to ask Bro twice. Later, Dad asked him if he liked the bike and when Bro told him he loved it, Dad said that he wanted him to have it and look after it for him once he was gone.

Dad wasn't overly sentimental so these words meant the absolute world to Bro. He swore to take care of it and ride it to all Dad's favourite spots, including The Duck Ponds, near West Head, where Dad wanted his ashes spread. Dad kept telling all his friends how proud he was that Dave was going to take care of his bike.

I really appreciated how open Dad was when talking about death. It was a harder pill for Bro to swallow but since Chump's death I had talked to Dad a lot about dying. I think I got my curious mind from Dad. We would often cry together and talk about where he was going to go and what it was going to be like, and whether there was anything at all beyond this life. I hate the thought of there being nothing so I don't entertain that one, but I loved how realistic Dad was. I think I get a lot of my coping mechanisms from him in regard to grief and death.

I can't remember ever seeing my dad cry before Chump died, but when he was on his last legs, it was like he couldn't stop crying. He cried at the sight of the sun, when we video-called his friends from bed and when we listened to music together. Dad was a tragic fan of The Rolling Stones; he played their music constantly and his all-time favourite song was 'Start Me Up'. Every time he'd get emotional, he used to say, 'You've made a grown man cry', riffing off the lyrics of his self-proclaimed anthem.

I asked my dad if he was afraid of dying. 'I'm not really scared anymore. Chump's already done it. I'll just go and hang out with him,' he said.

'You better send me a sign when you get up there, Dad,' I said. 'Show me through music, so I know you and Chump are getting weird and doing karaoke up there.'

That's how I wanted to picture them in the afterlife: on some cloud with beers, Dad holding his old wooden penis-shaped bottle opener as a microphone, and Chump hogging the stage doing the longest guitar solos.

I've never missed Chumpy more than when my dad was dying. All I wanted to do was fall into Chumpy's arms and ask him for his advice and wisdom. He was the person I turned to for help, the person who answered all of my silly questions and who listened to me even when I was talking rubbish. I just wanted to talk to Chumpy again and to hear him say, 'It's going to be okay, El. It's going to be okay.'

If words were too much to ask for, I would've settled for a cuddle. Bro and I just really needed Chump.

After a couple of weeks at Dad's bedside, I packed Minnie into the car and drove her forty-five minutes across Sydney. We were going to meet her other set of grandparents. Sal was in hospital, fighting cancer. I didn't expect to be introducing Minnie to Chris and Sal in a hospital, but then again, I didn't expect most of what had happened to me in the last couple of years.

It was a painful blow that both my dad and Chumpy's mum were so unwell at the same time. How much more shit could the universe throw at us? My heart ached for Sal, who was in the wars, but also for Chris. He and Sal are such a close unit. If she was down, he was in the trenches with her. I can't even imagine how much it would have hurt him to sit beside Sal's hospital bed all day, every day, for six months.

When I told Chris I wanted to bring Minnie to the hospital to meet them, he told me to message him when I parked and he would come and collect me from the carpark to take me upstairs. The hospital was a maze and he didn't want me to get lost. But I was on a mission: I wanted Chumpy's parents – Minnie's grandparents – to meet their first grandchild at the same time together. I found my way and pushed Minnie's stroller into Sal's room to surprise them. They were both sitting on the bed when we arrived. Minnie was asleep in the pram and as soon as we stepped inside, I picked her up and placed her in Sal's arms. It was so freaking cute. Honestly, we were all speechless for a good five minutes. There were no words. Sally was holding her grandchild, Chumpy's daughter, his Minnie-me.

She and Chris just kept looking at me, then to Minnie,

and back to me. When we eventually did speak, it was through tears. 'Wow, El. Would you look at this,' Chris said, shaking his head in total awe.

Chris and Sally gave me my life's greatest gift in Chumpy. As if that wasn't enough, they helped me to have Minnie by giving me their blessing, support and love. They are the salt of the earth.

My dad always had the last laugh. He was a larrikin until the end. For his final performance, he defied all odds and stuck it to the doctors who said he wouldn't live to Christmas in 2020. He made it to Christmas the following year as well, no doubt to prove everyone wrong.

My dad died on 27 January 2022. He was sixty-eight. He would've kicked himself for not making it to sixty-nine and missing out on a year of dirty jokes.

The date Dad died happened to be his mother's – my Oma's – birthday. If it wasn't so awful, it might have been poetic. I was holding him so tight when he left the Earth. For hours, Bro and I sat and talked to him. We told him he was our hero and that we loved him.

'You can let go, Dad. You can do it. We're here. We love you,' we said over and over again. I saw my dad take his last breath. I watched the life leave his body and his energy move on.

I can still see what my dad looked like after he died. After he stopped breathing, he was still there for a few minutes ... then he was gone. His body was no longer him; it was an empty vessel.

I'd had sixteen months to prepare for my dad's death. I knew it was coming – there was no stopping it – but when it finally did happen, it still came as a shock. I didn't expect it. I wanted to feel relieved that he wasn't suffering in pain anymore, but I just felt unprepared. I wasn't ready for him to go. I would never be ready for him to go.

A couple of days after Dad passed away, I walked into a café with my brother to get a much-needed coffee. Before we even had the chance to order, a song came on the sound system: 'Start Me Up' by The Rolling Stones. It was enough to make Bro, a grown man, and me, a grown woman, cry. I'd asked Dad to send me a sign that he was with Chumpy, and he did. It was gut-wrenching, but I was crying and smiling at the same time. More than anything, hearing that song gave me joy because I knew the two men I loved most were together.

Dad's funeral had a strict dress code: *Wear happy colours to celebrate Vluggy's life.* The Ann Wilson Chapel in Mona Vale was like a rainbow patchwork. It had been raining all week but, fittingly, the sun came out just for Dad that day. There was a guard of honour from his police colleagues and even a bagpipe player. At the start of the service, the MC made it clear we wanted the day to be a celebration. 'We know there's going to be tears, but can we also have clapping and laughing and cheering?' As funerals go, Dad's had its fair share of levity. The ceremony was still heartfelt, but it wasn't too earnest. A bit like Dad, really!

We got the funeral home to dress Dad in his sarong and a snorkel on his head, paired with his trademark crocs and socks and his trusty fishing rod, so he was ready for his next adventure in the beyond. That's how my dad was cremated – in all his glory.

Instead of flowers, we decorated Dad's coffin with Rolling Stones memorabilia, a guitar, his police hat and photos from the good old days. Dad's coffin wasn't a normal coffin, it was a special eco-friendly wood coffin with rope handles, like his own personal pirate ship. I stood up and spoke next to my brother. I'd left Minnie with a friend and she was watching the livestream of the funeral.

I opened my eulogy with a joke. 'Brace yourselves, everyone. I wouldn't be surprised if my dad jumped out of that coffin at any moment and told us that this was all a sick joke. We all know he loves a prank,' I said. A girl could dream.

The speeches that followed from Dad's mates and former colleagues all included stories of mischief, nudity and wild animals – lots of animals. On a NSW Police forum, people who worked with Dad back in the day shared their memories of him.

'I have a fond memory of a NSW Police Surfing Association competition we had one weekend in Ulladulla. It was the 90s and we all stayed at the Marlin Hotel. Vluggy was there with his pet snake. He wandered down to a pet shop and came back with a mouse. He proceeded to feed the mouse to his snake at the tables outside while we were having a beer.'

'RIP Pete. What a great bloke. I remember one morning on parade, an inspector chipped Pete about his hair being too long. The next day, he turned up bald as a badger and got in the shit for it.'

'Peter Vlug was the original "Crocodile Dundee" of the Northern Beaches. Snakes, lizards, spiders, turtles, dragons and many other creatures. Peter would check the surf, feed the lorikeets from the front veranda at Avalon, check out the koalas in the back yard then terrorise the locals. Many a time he was bitten by his beloved pythons, but he never gave up on them. A wonderful man, great friend and exceptionally good policeman.'

I shared my own tribute to my dad, with a photo of him with his arms wrapped around a toddler me and a lizard in our hands. I wrote:

Rest in Paradise Dadda,

You lit up our entire lives! We'd always turn to you for a laugh if ever we were down. As kids you'd cheer us up by handing us your phonebook and letting us prank call everyone in it. Every Saturday was Surf Safari day and we'd sing The Beach Boys en route to Freshie beach at the top of our lungs out the windows, begging for red lights so that the drive could take longer. Everything with you was so fun. You taught us to never grow up or take life too seriously.

You're our Tarzan, the strongest guy ever! You smashed your prognosis and whenever we would get upset watching you deteriorate, you'd say 'don't worry, be happy'.

We love you forever, Dad.

I'd become a pro at organising funerals. Big fucking sigh.

We held Dad's wake at the Warriewood Beach Surf Life Saving Club, overlooking the beach he'd called home for most of his life, the beach we grew up on. The beach where I had locked eyes with Chumpy on the stairs.

We thought Dad might like to have his ashes spread in the ocean – we thought wrong. He thought it might be bad for the fish, so he didn't want to be polluting the sea. Instead, Dad told us over and over again that he wanted to be set free at The Duck Ponds at McCarrs Creek in Ku-ring-gai Chase National Park. Dad used to ride his motorbike up there and go swimming in the fresh water. It would have been one of the last places he rode to before he had to give up his wheels.

The swimming hole is surrounded by thick bush, and Dad wanted his ashes to go into the soil. He wanted to give back to the Earth and hoped he'd be able to help the trees grow. Heaven knows with the amount of roadkill Dad ate, there'd be some nutrients in the ashes.

I've thought about putting some of Chumpy's ashes with Dad's out in the bush, so they're together in nature again. I know they'd both like that.

While Dad was dying, it felt like I had to set aside my grieving for Chumpy. I certainly didn't have the capacity to process losing both of them. It was hard not to draw comparisons between Chumpy's death and my dad's. Even though they happened under different circumstances, they were both still taken too soon. They were the two men I was closest to in the world and two of the brightest flames, and then they were gone.

I felt like grabbing my brother and never letting him go. 'You've got to stop doing stupid shit, Bro. I can't lose you too, I just can't,' I said, more than once.

Death brings out the very best and very worst in people. I have been very lucky that after losing Chumpy I only saw the good.

When Dad was dying, I couldn't cope with the stress. I had a newborn baby, was watching him slip away, was worried about my mother-in-law in hospital and trying to keep my head above water without Chumpy. I had to tap out. It was too much. I didn't have any space in my mind to deal with any added bullshit and there is so much paperwork and bureaucracy to deal with when someone is sick or dying. I felt awful, but I asked my brother to carry the mental load.

'Can you please take care of this, Bro? I can't. I just can't,' I said. And he did. He's my rock. I'm so lucky to have my Bro beside me.

I felt like I was surrounded by death and sickness and soul-crushing sadness, but I had a force field protecting me. I was so wrapped up in baby land that I didn't have the time or energy to stress about things outside of my control. All I had to do was look into Minnie's eyes – Chumpy's eyes – to find hope. Minnie is such a blessing, always, but especially during that time. She was this tiny, floppy baby who couldn't lift her own head up, but she gave me all my strength. What a legend.

Minnie has been – and still is – the greatest distraction. Grieving Dad has been a totally different experience because I have Minnie. I'm still processing it all and I know that it will take time. I still have Chump and Dad's numbers in my favourites on my phone. Sometimes I call and leave voice notes to Chump to tell him what's going on and how I feel. But some days it feels like I've tricked myself into thinking my dad's still here. He's just in Sydney, going about his business, carrying baby possums in his pockets and hitting up the 2 for 1 steak night at the pub. The reality of his loss hits me when I go to call him, or when I see my brother, or when I picture the look on his face after he stopped breathing.

CHAPTER NINETEEN

What Tomorrow Holds

This week, I found a gluten-free brownie mix in our pantry. Chumpy bought it before he died. I know it's the same packet because I'd never buy a gluten-free baking kit, and I have a photo of Chumpy with it in our shopping cart at the supermarket. It was during the Great Toilet Paper Shortage of 2020, and I took a photo of Chumpy standing in front of the empty toilet paper aisle with a funny look on his face. We thought it was so weird people were panic buying toilet paper at the start of the pandemic and the photo said exactly that. It was classic Chump.

The gluten-free brownie mix is two years old now. I'll never be able to make the brownies, knowing Chumpy isn't with me to eat them. And I'll never be able to throw the packet out, knowing it's the last thing in our pantry that he bought. So the gluten-free brownie mix will sit on the shelf as another souvenir of Chumpy.

I don't know if I'm the luckiest girl in the world because I got to love Chumpy, or the unluckiest because I lost him.

If I could go back to a time in my life, I would go back to 10 November 2012, the night of Laura's twenty-first; the night I first kissed Chumpy on the dance floor. The start of our love story. If I could go back and do it all over again, I would. I'd choose Chumpy every time – even knowing that I couldn't change what was to come.

In 2021, I launched the Chumpy Pullin Foundation with an amazing board of team members who absolutely adored and idolised Chump, and we held the inaugural gala the year after. The Foundation raises money to support aspiring snowboarders who otherwise wouldn't have the means to compete in the sport. When Chumpy started snowboarding, he was an outsider. He didn't come from a wealthy family, he didn't go to a private school and he didn't have a ski lodge on the slopes. And somehow – because of his ruthless drive, his parents' endless support, Bob the snowmaker who gave him a lift up the mountain so he could train, and all the people who tossed him a gold coin when he was busking on the streets to raise money for a new board or to fund his next season – he became

Australia's first ever snowboarding World Champion. He didn't want to be the last, and he didn't want rich kids to be the only ones who could follow in his footsteps.

In Australia, it's especially hard to make it as a professional snow athlete and Chumpy used to worry about it becoming a dying sport Down Under. He was passionate about creating and supporting opportunities for more Australians to participate and grow through snow sports. He wanted to open doors for those who might never have been to the snow before and pave the way for our next World Champ.

At the 2022 Chumpy Pullin Foundation Gala, we raised over $100,000 to do just that. The event was the culmination of so many people's hard work, and their ongoing love for Chumpy. At the black-tie event, we auctioned off a Mick Fanning surfboard, one of Chumpy's helmets, a backstage pass to a Fisher DJ set, a surfing experience with our friend, pro surfer Laura Enever, and a new Harley-Davidson. It was a spectacular night celebrating the sport Chumpy dedicated his life to. It was also very sad.

The moment I walked into the event space and saw Chumpy's face blown up onto a huge banner, his eyes looking down at me, I lost my breath. I had to force myself not to cry because I had to make a speech and I needed to hold it together, because once the flood gates open, that's it. I kept it together for the whole night, but I couldn't look at my brother sitting at the table next to me – he was crying hysterically, and I knew if I made eye contact with him, I would break down too. Aside from Dad's funeral, I hadn't seen him this emotional since the day Chump left.

Everyone I spoke to on the night told me they could feel Chumpy's presence in the room. It was quite powerful. There were a lot of emotions, heaps of tears and plenty of belly laughs. It was so nice to be able to share the night with people who loved Chumpy. I think we all needed it.

At the Gala, Chumpy's aunty Jan, who is a writer and had just read an early version of this book for me, went up to my mum. Jan held her and thanked her for what she did that day on the beach and in the back of the ambulance. 'Thank you for being with him in that moment,' Jan said. It meant so much to Mum, and to me. Mum was there for Chumpy when I couldn't be, and I'll always be grateful for that.

Now I am a mum I have even more respect for mine. I don't think I properly appreciated how strong she is and how hard it must have been for her with two kids and no money. The way she looked after Chumpy that day and the way she looks after me and Minnie is epic. I know I tease her about being a 'Karen' – but she's everything.

At the 2022 Beijing Winter Olympics – the first Games since he passed – Chumpy was front of mind for many of the Australian athletes and officials. It was so touching to see how many sportspeople wanted to honour Chump. Cam Bolton called Chumpy his hero. '[He was] one of the most incredible people that I know I'll ever meet or ever come across,' Cam told the Seven Network. 'Chumpy drove us all to be better; always, always, always. And still does.'

Likewise, first-time Olympian Adam Dickson called Chumpy his biggest inspiration. 'He was always the one to look up to in the sport,' Adam said. 'He was the best in Australia and pretty amazing at everything he did.'

Snowboarder Tess Coady, who had a photo of her and Chumpy as her phone screensaver for years, dedicated her race to him. 'I'm really here today because of Chumpy and what he inspired me to do, so I'm super grateful for him,' she explained.

And fellow rising star Adam Lambert added, 'He's always there with us in every race ... We miss him, but he's still here.'

In the Channel Seven broadcast, Chumpy's good friend and gold medal-winning Olympian Lydia Lassila – who handed over the Australian flag to him at the Sochi Games – paid tribute to him with a beautiful speech on-air. 'Chumpy was larger than life. He was such a talented man in every single thing he touched. He had the midas touch in music, sport and everything, but he also had an ability to inspire and mentor and give to everyone around him,' she said. 'His loss is still a shock. I don't think that will ever wear off. It's left a huge void in everybody's hearts, but his spirit is still so strong and alive. We honour him every single day.'

Throughout his career, Chumpy mentored a number of up-and-coming snowboarders and became an inspiration to many more in Australia and beyond. Chumpy is the reason so many people are where they are in the world. Me included. I am where I am today because of Chumpy, because of the life we created together and the devastating loss he left behind. This book is as much his as it is mine. My story is his; it's ours.

Chumpy's loss has brought me more pain than I ever thought I could survive and an ache in my heart that will never dull. But it's also brought me a new purpose in a way, in my mission to raise awareness about sperm retrieval and as a mum to Minnie. I know I wouldn't have had my new purpose if things didn't happen the way they did, and it helps me to focus on the silver linings rather than the dark clouds blocking the sun.

The *Darling, Shine!* podcast started as a way to share my journey and spread the word about post-mortem sperm retrieval. Since it launched just over a year ago, we've released three seasons, forty-odd episodes, and after only six months had over one million downloads. It started as a fun little project with my best mate Chloe, and it's become a bona fide community of extraordinary women and a successful business (even though, for me, deep down, it's still a fun little project with Chlo).

In 2022, a *Darling, Shine!* listener sent in a question asking us both how we cope with seeing the other one have what we want. Chloe still has the love of her life – Fisher – but she hasn't been able to have a baby yet. Meanwhile, I have a baby, but I don't have the love of my life. In early 2022, Chloe miscarried twin boys. It was her third miscarriage; she's lost four babies. As you would expect, both she and Fisher were devastated.

After Chloe lost the twins, I didn't really know what to do. All I wanted was to hold her and be with her, but I didn't know if bringing Minnie with me would be too painful. I told Chloe and Fisher I'd leave her at home, so she wasn't a trigger, and they said all they wanted was to see Minnie and cuddle her.

'Please bring Minnie over, please,' Fisher said. That's how beautiful they are.

There's no envy between Chloe and me because we're both so grateful for what we've got – and for each other. We've both experienced loss, so we understand what the other is going through and can sympathise. When I see Chloe and Fisher madly in love, I only feel happiness for them. And when they see me with Minnie, it's the same.

We're so close and lean on each other so much. I always think, 'God, what would I do if I didn't have Chlo and Fish?' and I know Chloe thinks, 'What would I do if I didn't have Min and El?' What we've lost hasn't torn us apart; it's brought us together.

I turned thirty in May 2022. I was relieved to have a friend's wedding on the same day, so the attention wasn't on me and I didn't have to mark another milestone without Chumpy.

Before I lost Chumpy, we would have thrown a big bash at our house. We loved nothing more than having all of our mates around for drinks, playing music and lighting up the fire pit in the backyard. I know Chumpy would have made a huge deal out of my thirtieth – in the same way we did his. That didn't happen, and I'm okay with it. Having a birthday party at home without Chumpy wouldn't have been the same.

Instead, a couple of weeks after my birthday, I headed to Crescent Head to celebrate with a good group of friends, all our babies and dogs. There was still plenty of drinks, good music and a fire pit, but it was different. I wasn't trying to recreate birthdays of years gone by; I was making new memories.

It's really hard for me to imagine being thirty-two in just a couple of years, and then being older than Chumpy was when he died; it's not right that I will be older than Chumpy. It baffles me that time just keeps on ticking without him. That's never more obvious than when I look at Minnie and see how much she grows and changes every day.

I also see it when I look in the mirror. Sometimes I don't recognise my old self. I've changed in the biggest ways and the smallest. It's extraordinary how much you can take physically and mentally when you need to. I'm older – and have the wrinkles to prove it! – but I'm also more sure of myself than I've ever been in my life. I am who I am and I'm fucking proud of that person. I think grief has really shaped me in a bizarre way, I'll never be the same again.

Some days I feel so close to Chumpy, like it was only yesterday that he hugged me goodbye in our garage. Other days, he feels so far away, like an entire lifetime ago. There are also days where I feel like I made him up entirely – that it was all a wild dream.

The days when I feel close to Chumpy are the easiest. That's when I know I'm being present and living in the moment. It's when he feels out of reach that I know I've taken on too much and am stretching myself too thin. Sometimes I can go months being completely normal and busy and unaffected. Not feeling anything is more awful than being sad. The numbness comes with a wave of guilt.

Of course, I am broken, but not all the time. I don't cry myself to sleep every night or fall into a heap whenever something reminds me of Chumpy. For the most part, I'm just a regular busy mum with a little baby who needs to put the laundry away and take the dog for a walk and is hanging to open a bottle of wine some nights. When Chumpy first died, I worried that I was a robot. I still do. Even though I've had time to process what's happened, I'm still going in and out of shock.

Having fun can feel like a betrayal. Why should I be able to have a good time when Chumpy isn't here having a good time with me? How can I be laughing when my person is gone? What does it say about me if I go to a party and don't think about Chumpy for an hour? Those questions aren't helpful. Even if I never had another good time, if I stopped laughing forever and if I spent every waking minute thinking about Chumpy, it wouldn't bring him back. I'll never not be grieving my loss, but I have to draw the line somewhere. I've had to make a conscious effort to let myself enjoy life. I can't be miserable for the rest of my life. Chumpy wouldn't want that, and neither do I.

The thing that makes me cry without fail is the thought of losing Rummi, my first-born 'child'. That's my biggest fear. I think about it all the time – even though I wish I wouldn't – and it haunts me. I know I wouldn't have gotten through the last two years without her. She saved me. Everyone told me the dog gets pushed to the side when you have a baby, but that has definitely not been the case in our family. I think Rummi gets even more attention and love – and ear-pulling – now we have Minnie. We're always together, the three of us. Rummi comes everywhere with us.

I've never seen Minnie with Chumpy physically – they've never been in my eyes together, only my heart – but I have seen Rummi with him. I think that's why Rummi feels like a connection to him. When she goes, it'll be like losing the last living reminder of Chumpy, which I know isn't the case because Minnie is his daughter, but it'll still be excruciatingly hard. Since the day Chumpy brought Rummi home, she's been such an important part of my life, and now she's like the dog embodiment of Chumpy. They were so close, I swear they share a soul. When Rummi dies, part of me will die too.

On the flip side, it makes me so happy to think of Minnie growing up with Rummi in her life. They love each other already, but I know their friendship is going to grow as she gets older. Sometimes I'll catch them staring into each other's eyes and I'll wonder what they're thinking – and if Chumpy's involved in their deep, unspoken conversation.

This year, I can't stand the thought of marking the second anniversary of Chumpy's death, so on 7 July, I'm jumping on a plane with Minnie and Mum to Greece. We'll be in transit, up in the sky, somewhere over Europe when the 7th becomes the 8th and one year becomes two. I might wave out the plane window to Minnie's daddy in the sky.

Everyone copes with grief differently. I often feel lucky for being able to grieve in the way I have. I have a beautiful community of friends and family to lean on, Rummi to get me out of bed every morning and Minnie to keep me busy and give me hope for the future.

On the other hand, Chumpy's parents Chris and Sally are based in an isolated town on the south coast of New South Wales. They spend a lot of time alone with their grief and they've been dealing with Sal's cancer diagnosis. My heart aches for them. I know that no matter how much time passes, they'll never be okay. Nothing will ever be okay again. Even though I've only had a short amount of time with Minnie, I cannot imagine losing her. A parent losing a child is another world of pain.

I know my loss weighs heavily on them, on top of their own. I think it's hard for them to fathom me being on my own because they've been together from the second that they sat next to each other in that Valiant as teenagers. They haven't spent a single day apart – they don't even go to the grocery store without each other – so my being alone is entirely foreign to them.

Chumpy was my soulmate, but, in a totally different way, he was also his sister Emma's soulmate. They were kindred spirits. When Em came to visit us on the Gold Coast recently, she wore a matching t-shirt to Minnie's and they looked like the coolest aunty–niece duo of all time. We took Minnie to the local animal sanctuary and Em insisted on us seeing every single animal there. It was such a special day, but sometimes the greatest days are the hardest. The sweetness of every good moment leaves an aftertaste of longing – longing that Chump was there with us showing his daughter her first koala.

As much as I love Minnie and feel eternally grateful to have her, she's not a replacement for Chumpy. That isn't her burden to carry. She is her father's daughter, but she's so much more than that. She is her own person, and I can't wait to keep getting to know her and to continue to learn from her. Minnie has taught me so much already. I already knew what unconditional love was because of Chumpy, but Minnie has taken that to a completely new level. She is everything. I'm so lucky to be her mum.

Since I've had Minnie, I get asked quite regularly if and when I'll have another baby. Of course, it's something I've thought about and there's a comfort in knowing I have another embryo left, but it's not something I've had time to seriously contemplate. My life with Minnie is so full and busy. We're such a good little team, it's hard to imagine adding another child to the mix in the near future. She's enough. I'm whole. Then again, who knows what the distant future holds? Heck, who knows what tomorrow holds?

I was in a clothing store with a friend the other day when the owner – who I know – asked me if I was going to try out online dating now that's it been nearly two years since Chumpy passed. The friend I was with went pale and her jaw dropped – she couldn't believe someone had just asked me such a personal question – but I was happy to answer it. I've been such an open book with my story, and talking about Chumpy and sharing my emotions has been a form of therapy for me. Even if what I say doesn't make sense all of the time, I never want Chumpy to be the elephant in the room.

To answer the shop owner's question, I used a lot of 'ums' and 'ahs,' and took a lot of pauses. I know that, at some point, I will date again. I'm thirty, and I can't imagine spending the rest of my life alone. In saying that, I can't imagine being with anyone other than Chumpy either. I still feel like he's just away overseas and that he'll be back one day. I know deep down that's not true, but that's how it feels.

Right now, I'm not ready to date. I don't have room emotionally to think about a romantic relationship. All of my love is going to Minnie and Rummi and that suits me just fine.

I like to think of the heart as the muscle it is. No-one will ever be able to fill the space in my heart that Chumpy holds; I will always love him. Always. I hope that one day my heart will be able to grow to love another. I didn't think I could love anyone as much as Chumpy, then we got Rummi … and then I had Minnie. Love isn't one or the other. I'll never 'move on' from Chumpy, but I can move forward. Whether that's with someone or on my own, I don't know.

When it comes to Minnie, she will always know who her dad is. Even if another man comes into our lives, he will never take Chumpy's place. That's simply not possible. Chumpy is Minnie's dad. Minnie is Chumpy's daughter. The end.

I still write letters to Chumpy in my mind. This is the latest:

Dear Chump,

I still can't believe this is true. I miss you.

I wish you could see Minnie and hold her. She's perfect. She's you all over. I know she's wise like you, I can tell when I look into her eyes. It's like looking into your eyes. She's everything we dreamed of.

We had our first Mother's Day yesterday. I know you would have made me endless coffees and pancakes and followed me around the house with your guitar improvising songs all morning.

Rummi's been the best co-parent ever, she's obsessed with her lil sis. She panics when Minnie's not with us. She's always looking for her. Just like she still wanders the house searching each room for you.

Mornings are still our sweet spot… cuddles in bed, coffee and beach walks. For you, always. We've actually been family-bonding in the car of an afternoon when Minnie's having her witching hour, we blast your music and sing and cry together. Rummi being her usual backseat driver, barely blinking in case she misses something. She still stands up in the boot of the car the entire nine-hour drive to Sydney. Those road trips suck without you.

You know all this. I know you're watching us and guiding us. I hope I am making you proud baby.

I love you,

Elmo

Every morning, I wake up, grab Minnie from her cot in the nursery and bring her into my bedroom. We open the blinds and look out of the window to the horizon – the same horizon Chumpy looked at on 8 July 2020, on the same spot he saw it was a glorious day, and in the same room he decided to go spearfishing to make the most of it.

Every morning, I hold Minnie in my arms and we look out the window together. 'Good morning, world. Hello, Daddy in the sky,' I say, pointing towards the horizon. 'Your daddy's up there, Minnie. Look at the sun shining down on us.'

Every morning, we start the day by acknowledging Chumpy. It's our ritual, our wake-up routine, our moment of stillness together before we jump into the day with the same energy Chumpy lived his life.

If not with Chumpy, then for him.

)em for Chumpy

Inspired by Emma

By Aunty Jan

We saw the rainbow on the beach the day you left
Sunsets so golden each day after
The giant water spouts off the coast of Wollongong

Was that you waving at Em?

The black cockatoos flying overhead
The bark they dropped on the track as we came down
    the mountain

Did they call your name?

The small shrine we left in a cave high on the
    escarpment
Red tea-light candles and incense stolen from your
    auntie's house
An arrangement of gum leaves, moss, wild flowers
    and bracken

Did you find it?

We stand on the ocean cliff watching the huge swell
    coming down the coast.
At your old stomping ground, the surf is pumping.
Waves 11.5 metres high.

Did you send them?

If you can't go home
We won't go either
Into the bush we'll walk every day
To feel your breath as our breath
To hear your song on the wind
To catch your smile in the shimmer of a golden leaf
As it prepares to dive into the gully

ACKNOWLEDGEMENTS

From Ellidy

I'm currently sitting in Ibiza, Spain, writing the final touch for this book – the thank yous. I feel so incredibly blessed with the amazing people in my corner.

Firstly, thank you Chlo and Fisher for being by my side every moment, flying Minnie and I over here to live and travel with you for the European summer, showing her unconditional love and taking her on as though she's your own.

I cannot thank Nada Herman, Hachette Australia, Vanessa Radnidge and Alley Pascoe enough for giving me this opportunity and listening to my endless stories. Alley, you brilliantly captured what Chumpy meant to so many of us. Thank you to Christa Moffitt for the stunning cover, and Hachette's finest; Stacey Clair, Caitlin Murphy, Isabel Staas, Lillian Kovats, Chris Sims, Kelly Gaudry, Emily Lighezzolo, Bethany Nevile, Fiona Hazard, Louise Stark, Melissa Wilson, and all the Hachette Australia team.

I started listing everyone – Mai Mai, Lizzo, Lorbs, Luce, Ren, Dani, Shorty, Beccy, Elly, Elba, Nic, Corbs, Tashy, Lizey, Tiffy, Elly, Bells, AJ, Mads, Shimmy, Lotte and GG – and then I realised I am going to miss someone so I am going to say … My girls, you know who you are.

I am so lucky to have the friends that I do. Many, many special people didn't get a mention in this book. I want to especially thank Big T and Hannah for being by my side every single day; LJ and Ezzle for your advice always, and for proofreading this book and workshopping parts with me; and Maddy and Jourdy for having my back and always looking out for me from afar no matter what. Thank you!

To Chump! My love, thank you for choosing me. And growing with me. I was just a kid when I met you, and a grown-ass woman when you left. You opened my eyes, taught me to be present and gave me the world. Thank you for showing me the most unique and unwavering rock-solid love that is ours only. I'll cherish it forever. I would choose you over and over. I'd do it again, and again, even knowing the pain of losing you, because having you for almost a third of my life makes me the luckiest person ever.

Thank you to Chris, Sal, and Em ... You're stuck with me. Family forever!

Thank you to Mum and Bro TIMES A BILLION. I wouldn't be doing any of this without you. And my Dadda ... My shining star up there forever, with Chump. I find comfort in knowing that you have one another. I hope you're having a beer somewhere amazing and looking down smiling.

My dog, Rummi! Chumpy may have loved you even more than he loved me. I look at you and my heart feels like it melts. You feel every single emotion with me and haven't left my side through it all. You are the best sidekick and therapist I could ever ask for.

Thank you to Leanne Laydon and to Aunty Jan for allowing me to include your poems in this book. You're crazy-talented. Thank you to Thomas Wielecki for your photo.

Thank you to Kathy and Em at Chic, Andrea Keir, Denham Hitchcock and the Spotlight team, Remy Rippon at *Vogue* and Britt at *Darling, Shine!*

Thanks to everyone who has supported The Chumpy Pullin Foundation and especially the advisory board of Ryan Tiene, Ben Johnson, Ben Wordsworth, Ben Rennie, Laura Enever, Peter Ferras, Jackson Holtham, Kristen Guseli and Shelly Morgan. And to Kyle Bullock and Mick Fanning for your kind hearts, and all Chumpy's friends, teammates and sponsors, especially Red Bull.

The love and support I received after Chump passed, and again with the birth of our daughter, is unbelievable. The community at my hometown on the Northern Beaches of Sydney and my forever home on the Gold Coast is something really special. Big shout-out to my neighbours who are literally on 24/7 speed dial and drop everything for me, you're never allowed to move away!

People are incredible. I feel the love and support deeply.

– Love Minnie, Rummi and me

From Chris and Sally Pullin

Our home, the then small town of Mansfield, was a warm and friendly community. The kids called it Mansvegas. My mum and dad lived nearby in Bonnie Doon, and Sal's in Alexandra. We had the snow, the lake and the bush; it was all so good. Together with our friends the Oliveries – Pete, Linda and their four kids – we had some awesome times camping and hanging out. And the music played by Chumpy, Emmi and Zigi was loved by the town as if it was part of its identity. It was a fantastic time for us.

After we lost Chumpy, our letterbox overflowed for weeks. Most of the cards and letters were from Mansvegas – from lovely people who just couldn't believe this news, who hated hearing this news, who felt so very sorry for Sally, me, Emmi and Elli.

Thank you to all the people who shared those happy, crazy, loving years.

– The Pullins

FURTHER READING AND RESOURCES

The Chumpy Pullin Foundation
chumpypullinfoundation.org

Darling, Shine! Podcast
darlingshine.com

If you need to seek support for any issues covered in this book, please contact one of the services listed below. In an emergency, please call 000.

Lifeline Australia
lifeline.org.au | 13 11 14

Lifeline Aotearoa
lifeline.org.nz | 0800 543 354

Beyond Blue
beyondblue.org.au | 1300 22 46 36

Headspace
headspace.org.au

The grief workbook that Lotte and I put together, *Now What? A Guide to Navigating Life After Loss*, is available now at the link below.

Now What? comprises 110 pages of comprehensive grief support, including journal prompts, worksheets and downloadable meditations.

As you work through the book, you'll learn how to build a self-care toolkit, cultivate positive habits, create routine, navigate your relationships, connect to your spirituality, record your memories, and discover new resources and support in the midst of your loss.

Visit the website for more information:
nowwhatgrief.com